T0370527

Snapshots of God's Caring Presence

HEARTWARMING AND INSPIRATIONAL SHORT STORIES

Raymond J. Golarz

With Marion Simpson Golarz

authorHOUSE®

AuthorHouse™
1663 Liberty Drive
Bloomington, IN 47403
www.authorhouse.com
Phone: 833-262-8899

Published by AuthorHouse 05/13/2024

ISBN: 979-8-8230-2580-5 (sc)
ISBN: 979-8-8230-2579-9 (e)

Library of Congress Control Number: 2024908559

Print information available on the last page.

Dedicated to

my wife Marion
and
my older brother who
died before we got to know him

Contents

Foreword

This collection of short stories gives witness to Ray Golarz's deep belief in the presence of God—a God who, in his words, "sits on our shoulder and whispers to those of us who are willing to listen about the good we can do when we sense potential evil, predictable tragedy, or just the opportunity to make someone's life better."

Those of you who have followed this author's writings will recognize some of these stories. They are included here because they particularly send the message that we are not alone—there is a never-ending caring presence.

Drawing upon his own life experiences and the life experiences of others, especially those people who have dedicated their lives to helping others, the author sees these stories as moments where God is subtly revealed. For Ray Golarz they are moments that cannot be explained by logic, serendipity, or coincidence.

These are not stories that embody any particular faith tradition, nor are they akin to children's stories about the magical existence of Santa Claus. They are, however, infused with what we talk about when we use that phrase, God was there.

However, any reader, even those who are not interested in this discussion of God's role in our lives, should not pass on the opportunity to be moved by the courage and goodwill of people who try to overcome evil, soften the pain of tragedy, lift the burden of overwhelming challenges, and make this world a kinder place to live in—with the ever-present hand of God.

MJG

Preface

My father was a storyteller—a great storyteller. I could listen to him forever, even when I had heard the story from him before. When I began teaching, I followed his lead. Therefore, much of my teaching was in story form.

In the mid-1980s, I had the chance experience to keynote a conference because the scheduled keynoter was sick. So, despite inadequate preparation, I told stories. Surprisingly, the audience really enjoyed them. Thus, I got asked to keynote more and more conferences.

My audiences were always people in the helping professions—teachers, parents, police officers, counselors, psychologists, and social workers. It didn't take me long to discover that what they were looking for was a keynote filled with stories that would uplift or inspire them. Their work was such that they needed to understand that they were not alone out there. It wasn't their hand alone working to make a difference.

So I never stopped doing that. The only variation was that I added more and more stories. When I was concluding my keynoting career, I began to get requests for the stories in written form. I felt bad. I had never written them. I just presented them from my scribbled notes and memory.

It was my wife Marion who pushed me to write them. I had already had the experience of writing a number of books, but moving from a story told in a keynote to one that was written was a bit tricky. Since the time that I began writing these stories, a number have appeared in USA Today, Yahoo news, and some in recently published books. Some have never appeared anywhere in print.

Though my stories, written over the years, have sometimes covered an array of topics, the stories chosen for this book were specifically selected because I believe that they are not only uplifting and inspirational, but because I believe that God's presence is integral to each story. He is sometimes in the wings backstage, but other times His work and presence is right up in your face.

Without deep explanation, a terse review of the table of contents will give you a glimmer of what I mean.

Beginning with the first story, "Lord when did we see You,,,?" You will encounter God's close presence. When you get to the fourth story, *Mike the Bus driver,* God is certainly there, but He is more in the wings. There is virtually no story where God is not present. His location simply varies.

My suggestion to you as a reader is that you not read the book in one setting. It's not that you couldn't, but the book is not presented to you as a full meal. Rather it's intended to come to you as a series of appetizers. Then again, how you ingest is certainly up to you.

Bon appétit.

"Lord, when did we see You. . .?"

Matthew 25: 37-40 (NKJV)

O ne very beautiful mid-October Friday, we left home and headed north to Evanston, Illinois. Our two oldest sons were playing football on Saturday for Northwestern University. We got there around 5:00 p.m., did a bit of unpacking, and then headed downstairs to the hotel restaurant for a quiet meal. Outside of the restaurant windows we could see that the trees on both sides of the street were ablaze with their fall colors, and the evening touches of sunlight were performing magic with their leaves. At meal's end my youngest son Tom and I headed outdoors for an evening walk. After going a fair distance, we turned the corner at McDonald's and found that the sidewalk was fairly crowded.

Out of the corner of my eye, I caught sight of a homeless man. He had his left hand out and cupped, while with his right hand he held together his lightweight, tattered, and zipper-less jacket. He was very unkempt, and next to him on the ground was a bundle tied together at the top with a stick. I found myself drawn to and looking directly at him as his eyes locked unswervingly on me in a deep and profoundly peaceful way. I remember at that moment saying to myself, "Why not, I can afford a buck or two."

I was sure I had some cash. I reached into my pocket and was pleasantly surprised. As I neared the homeless stranger, I pulled the cash out and looked into my right hand—two twenties. I looked down at Tom. He didn't seem to know what was going on, so I slowly and somewhat shamefully pocketed the money. Then Tom and I headed back toward the hotel. I remember affirming to myself: "How can I give him a twenty or two twenties? It's unreasonable. No one would expect me to give him that much." I tried to calm my conscience.

After our short walk back, I reached into my pocket and then stopped dead in my tracks. The money was gone. I looked down at Tom and without explaining to him said, "Quick, Tom, we need to go back."

I knew we wouldn't find the money but I had to look. As we walked quickly, I could see through the half-crowded sidewalk ahead of us the homeless stranger coming our way. He was slowly waving his hand in the air. Soon I could hear him saying, "Sir, Sir, you dropped these." Crumpled in his waving hand were my twenty dollar bills. He continued, "I found them right after you left, but couldn't keep up with you and the boy."

As I looked into his eyes, I remembered why I had been compelled to look his way in the first place. It was his eyes. They were so deep, peaceful and caring—so calm and gentle. They belied the rest of his appearance. His eyes were not homeless at all. They were filled with a caring presence.

Sheepishly, I said, "Sir, would you please keep the money?"

"Only if you really wish it."

"I do."

"Then I will."

He smiled that very calm smile, looked again into my eyes, then turned and walked away.

Later I took a walk by myself to look for the man with eyes that seemed to calm me and bring me a strange peace. Though I asked many, no one could help me. No one strangely could ever remember seeing him. All I do know is that whoever he was, he seemed peacefully at home in our world—more at home than most I have ever met or known.

Lord, could it be that it's we who are the homeless and needy wanderers?

The Lasting Beauty
of Compassion

By noon my brother Joe, age 10 and I, age 12, had finished our first round of caddying for the day. We had eaten our baloney sandwiches and were starting a game of mumblety-peg with our knife. Some 30 yards behind us, older caddies were running toward a group that was forming. There appeared to be some kind of fight. Finally, a break in the crowd allowed us to see, though not clearly. One big white kid that we had never seen had a much smaller black kid forced to his knees. He was pulling the kid's face to his crotch. The little guy was fighting back, crying and screaming, but two other big white kids were restraining him. Then with great force the big kid, hit the little guy squarely in the face with a clinched fist. Blood from the small kid's face seemed to splash everywhere. He hit the ground hard. Several other kids started kicking him and laughing hysterically as he attempted to escape. One kicked him squarely on the side of the head.

I looked over at my little brother Joe and could see tears streaming down his face. Neither of us had ever seen such brutality and hostility—nothing even close. I looked back and saw the little black kid finally break loose and run in the direction of the railroad tracks some 200 yards away. I looked for Joe, but he was gone. Then, out of the corner of my eye, I could see my brother running after the kid. I screamed out Joe's name and then ran behind him past the soaring bricks being thrown by the gang members. For some reason, they weren't following. Soon we neared the tracks. Now it was just the kid, my brother Joe, and me. As the kid approached the tracks, he grabbed a big stone, turned, and screamed at Joe, "Don't come any closer or I'll throw it." Joe stopped and just stood there for a moment looking at the kid whose face and shirt were covered in blood. He wasn't very big, kind of skinny really, but taller than Joe. Joe then did something I'll forever remember. He started walking slowly toward the kid. Somewhat startled, the kid backed up, falling across the first railroad track and screamed again, "I'll throw it. I mean it. I'll throw it."

Joe slowed but continued coming. Then Joe stopped and opened his arms wide. A moment passed and then slowly the rock dropped from the kid's hand. Weeping uncontrollably, he fell into Joe's arms. They were together draped across the track. Joe held the boy's bleeding head and face against his chest. Then he looked up at me with what, for me, looked like the eyes of Christ. Soon an inexplicable peace and holy calm gently surrounded the two of them. Joe continued to hold him until the boy slowly let go. When finally he left us, he walked down the tracks. Some distance away he turned, stopped, and waved. We waved back.

Years later, Joe and I were returning home in his old run-down Ford from a night in Old Town-Chicago. Car trouble forced a stop at an obscure out of the way Chicago South Side gas station. We got out. Almost immediately, six or seven tough looking black guys surrounded us. It was a terrifying moment. Then the biggest guy slowly and very inquisitively moved to a position face to face with Joe.

Though years had passed, their recognition of one another was almost immediate. He smiled as did Joe, and then he said to the others, "Fix his car. He's my brother." Joe and he embraced for a moment, and then they went and sat on a curb and talked. As we drove home that early morning, Joe and I did not speak—words seemed unnecessary.

His face simply emanated that holy calm that I had seen on the tracks so many years before.

My Friend Jose, God, and the Rolling Mill

Whenever I wash and dry my hands, the inside of my right wrist becomes visible to me as does the scar that remains there from the deep cut across that wrist. The flashback is immediate as is the vivid memory of my friend Jose and God's caring presence.

Jose and I met while members of the labor gang in the rolling mill at Inland Steel. We soon developed the habit of having lunch together on the loading dock, he with his tacos and tamales and me with my baloney and mustard sandwiches.

Most days we worked together. Then one day I was assigned away from the labor gang and Jose. My assignment was at the other end of the rolling mill where we never worked. Specifically, I was assigned to work alone in front of a stack of thin-grade steel sheets that were about four feet square. I was to lift one sheet at a time, hold the sheet up to a light and look for pin holes. Heavy duty gloves and arm guards were essential, for the sheets were thin and sharp. Sheets with pin holes went on a stack to my left and those without pin holes on the stack to my right. After two hours you developed a rhythm, after four hours boredom set in, and after six hours, a new stack of steel sheets arrived.

It was about 10:00 A.M. in the morning. The rhythm portion of the day was ending and I was moving toward boredom. Then I heard an intense, loud sound of something like massive steel- on-steel materials falling. The wall of steel sheets in front of me and the steel barrier behind the sheets were being crushed and strewn about like confetti. I remember being struck. Then all went black.

The next thing I remembered was the smiling face of Jose.

"You will be OK. God sent me."

I turned my head and could see blood everywhere. I must have looked frightened for Jose then said, "Do not be afraid, I stopped the bleeding. God sent me."

I passed out again.

Later that day in the clinic I learned that a large fork lift had backed into piles of steel, pushing those piles into the steel sheets and my work area. The accident resulted in a head injury and a slash across the inside of my right wrist from one of the steel sheets. I had been bleeding a lot, but Jose had found me, and had rigged a tourniquet and stopped the bleeding. Several others had been in the area before Jose but had not seen me under the stacks of steel.

At lunch on the dock the following week I asked Jose, "Tell me what happened."

He replied, "We did not have enough shovels so they sent me to get more."

"But Jose the shovels are stored on the other side of the plant, nowhere near where I was working."

"I know, but God told me to go that way and find you, so I followed where He told me to go."

As he spoke, I can still remember feeling that a loving presence was near.

It's probable that I would not have been found in time if it were not for Jose. How he found me and why he looked remains understandable only if you believe. His gift to me was more than my continued temporal life. He reaffirmed my faith.

The Bible tells us that Christ asked Peter to come out and walk on the water. After taking several steps Peter sank. I am quite confident that Jose would have made it to the boat. Such, I believe, was his unwavering faith and what I came to judge was God's reciprocal love for him.

As I said earlier, whenever I wash and dry my hands, the inside of my right wrist becomes visible to me as does the scar that remains there from the deep cut across my wrist. The flashback is immediate as is the vivid memory of my friend Jose and what I believe was God's caring presence.

Mike the Bus Driver

As I traveled our country keynoting conferences, I found often that I came away with more than I gave. Once, in North Carolina, a young lady who had been in my audience gave me the gift of the following story about Mike, a school bus driver.

His assignment was bussing children grades one through four. He liked his work—he liked kids. Earlier in life he had been a military fighter pilot. A war injury ended his service, but Mike had no regrets. Driving a bus and daily seeing young faces was a good life.

One day a senior administrator asked him to deliver a note to the building librarian. Mike accidently entered an auditorium where a faculty meeting was in progress. Leaving would have caused a disruption, so he sat down quietly. He intended to leave as soon as he could. He heard the principal express a deep concern. "My colleagues, many of our students seem not to appreciate their good work. I know you are aware of this, for you have expressed such to me. I have no immediate answer, so I ask you to assist me in any way you can with some resolution."

The meeting ended and Mike quietly left. Though simply a bus driver, he thought possibly he might help. He had noted for quite some time how his students often left their graded school work on the bus. It had saddened him particularly to see so many of the papers with stars and smiley faces strewn across the floor. He knew, of course, why they left them, for he knew his route. Most of his students went home to empty houses, so there was no one to show such papers to.

Mike decided to do what he thought could be his part. He announced to all of the students riding his bus that Mike wanted to see their good work—especially the work with the stars and smiley faces. Then, when he looked at their papers and had expressed appropriate complements for their work, he would sign, "Mike" in the upper right hand corner of their paper with what he called, "his Magic Christmas red pen." Soon Mike found that at the end of his evening run, the bus was much less littered. There were never again papers on the floor bearing stars and/or smiley faces. Teachers began to notice children requesting more of such rewards and their willingness to work for them. It didn't take teachers long to find the source of enthusiasm. It did take a little longer for Mike to load his late afternoon bus run, but everyone seemed willing to work around that.

Eventually Mike passed away. The number of young children and parents who came to his funeral was inspiring. Shortly after his death, a bizarre practice began to occur with no known perpetrators. Affectionate graffiti began to show up on the bus Mike drove, always in red and always a star or smiley face. An authority never looked for the perpetrators, nor was the graffiti ever washed or wiped off. Over time the graffiti simply faded away.

My story teller then told me her name and advised me that she was a teacher at the school. Then without saying anything else, she pulled from her purse an old yet neatly folded paper—one of her own work products from her own childhood so many years ago.

The folded paper exhibited a star, a smiley face, and the name "Mike" written in the upper right-hand corner--a name written, I'm sure, with a "Magic Christmas red pen." She looked up at me and smiled. I nodded my head slowly and smiled back.

The Treasure Box

S ome teachers are artists who can open the treasure box of profound learning masterfully. Such was Mr. Nelson. He taught poetry and literature. The poem he selected that first week of class was "Thanatopsis."

I recall vividly how he enthusiastically passed out printed sheets of the poem while he danced between the aisles of our classroom chair--simultaneously sharing in his mellow baritone voice stanza after stanza of Bryant's magnificent poetic gift. With each reading he seemed to go deeper into the poem. It was as if the poem and he were now in a conversation. It was clear that he had created magic. He took us far that day. He had opened a treasure box and invited us to glimpse inside. We had, however, no idea of the depth of the trip he was planning for us.

A week later he took us further. Using the poem, he had us carefully ponder, discuss, and analyze. He guided us into an open conversation of mortality. Finally, cognitively exhausted, we understood Bryant. Or so we thought. But he wasn't finished. He looked at us and said, "My young friends, I have but one final question." We eagerly awaited, confident and cognitively ready. Then he said, "In the manner and mode of Bryant's poem, what would you do if your mother died?" It seemed a strange question and momentarily he caught us off guard, but we regrouped. Hands going up, responses came from all corners of the room: "I'd call other members of my family, they would need to know." "I'd search for insurance papers—we'd need those." "I would quickly write the essential obituary."

While we gave our answers Mr. Nelson had been moving slowly to the, right-front-seat in our classroom, a seat occupied by Tony. Tony seldom said much. We all knew he was kind of slow, but no one ever laughed at him. He was perceived as just a big, not-very-bright, nice kid. We had finished our responses just as Mr. Nelson arrived at Tony's chair. I remember that he looked directly into Tony's face and in a quiet, gentle voice, he asked, "Tony, what would you do?"

Tony quietly responded, "I'd cry." Mr. Nelson looked up at all of us as the room fell silent. The lid of the Treasure Box had been opened wide by a "not too bright" kid named Tony, and an artist named Mr. Nelson who, in the silence of that classroom, watched as we all now peered in. He then said, "Bryant meant not for you to intellectually ponder death. Rather, he meant for you to feel. The journey into the poem was not meant to be a cognitive journey—rather a journey to be felt—a conversation not of minds, but of hearts. Now you may leave class early. Walk the grounds and ponder what you may have learned today."

We left class richer that day. Somehow, in that brief moment in that classroom, an artist named Mr. Nelson showed us where to find our real humanity, and he did it through the magic of poetry and by pointing out for us the incredible beauty and wisdom existing within, what we had thought, was one of the simpler of our fellow men.

Several of us walked Tony home from school that day where we got to meet his mom and dad. We began to include him in some of our activities—like football games and some of our activities in the park.

Tony seemed to like that—he seemed to just kind of like being included.

One of God's Favorite Places

I grew up three houses away from a long and narrow empty field above which were high electrical wires. The wires were held up by enormous sixty-foot steel structures which gave the appearance of a parade of giant robots.

As children we named this field below these steel structures, "The Weeds." The far border of this field was the railroad tracks. Many rocks, small gullies, an array of trees, wild flowers and prairie grasses were everywhere in this field. It was alive with creatures and bugs of all kinds. Our parents permitted us to play here but we were never to leave the weeds and venture over the railroad tracks.

Alas, in the manner of Adam and Eve, we didn't listen. It didn't take long for us to sin and enter the "forbidden lands and taste of its fruits." Centuries ago, before these tracks were laid, there had existed small, long bodies of water named by the earliest residents as the Finger Lakes. Sadly, landfills, and the construction of warehouses, factories, and roads had all but eliminated the existence of these pristine lakes and the flora and fauna that surrounded them. What remained was but a shadow of that forgotten place. Yet, anyone who explored this remaining sanctuary with a child's imagination could share a scene that frontiersmen must have found in every part of our virgin country before man conquered and civilized the wilderness.

The trees around the now smaller remaining Finger Lakes area were larger than the trees found in The Weeds that were closer to home. The prairie grass flowers were of a wider array and their colors more intense. As we crossed the tracks and approached, animals of all kinds that had been comfortably sunning dove for the protection of the waters. These remaining little lakes were clear and were four to five feet deep. Along the edges were hundreds of tadpoles. The sand was white beach sand, for this area had in its distant past been the shore of Lake Michigan.

Thousands of these treasure spots still remain across our country. They are, sadly, missed or forgotten by most adults. We see only a muddy pond or a dirty, wet place at the end of the railroad tracks where the eyes of little children, as we all once were, see the treasure. Because of their childhood innocence these places call to them to come, splash, touch, and play.

Though I was always captivated when I ventured into these forbidden lands, it was my little sister Barbara who seemed most taken. Often, as her smiling face looked up from her bare-footed squatting position at a tiny lake's water's edge, she would ask, "Ray, is this one of God's favorite places?"

"Yes," I would reply.

"I knew it, I knew it. I knew it. It's mine too, Ray. It's mine too."

Then with her face overflowing with joy and using her little child's fingers, she would gently stroke the water, quietly hum and watch the tadpoles scurry to different places—places I'm sure that only she, the angels and God talked about.

I am convinced that this was one of God's favorite places. I am convinced because I believe that it was here that He knew He could always come, talk, and play with his angels and the little girl so full of joy—my little sister.

So, my dear friends, before the sands complete their travel through your hour glass, revisit your "Rosebud" once more, and play with the your tadpoles, your angels and your God.

Remember, it's His favorite place too—a place that you will assuredly feel His caring presence.

Marble Street

The steel processing plant was on Marble Street. It had been twelve years since I had seen a co-worker in that plant get his arm crushed up to his elbow by a press. As I turned now onto the street, I could still clearly recall his screams. God, how we all wanted him to pass out.

Now, however, having completed college and a master's degree I was back on Marble Street. I was a young administrator in charge of a newly-formed poverty prevention program. No longer did I wear metatarsal work boots, stuff work gloves in my back pocket, or carry a metal lunchbox—all had been replaced by a white shirt and tie.

In those bygone years I had never noticed the row of run down, unpainted houses across the street from the steel plant. I would now soon be walking down a half flight of concrete stairs into one of several basement apartments in a dilapidated 1880 structure.

With me was Fred. Fred was head of intervention services for the inner city. He was formidable—a six-foot-three, 240 pound barrel-chested powerhouse. We were on the hunt for a twelve year old girl who was reported as having no adult care or supervision. She had been spotted foraging for food in garbage cans. We got to a door in the darkened area at the bottom of the stairs. Fred knocked. No response. The door was slightly ajar so Fred pushed it open. Immediately roaches scurried everywhere. One step in and we were inundated by the smell of rot, decay, and the overpowering smell of vomit and urine.

Acclimating to the dark, we could now see movement on the floor in the corner of the room. Cowering there was a half-clad, very thin, and dirty little girl. She was clearly terrified. Fred, the father of children that age stood there as tears streamed down his face. He then declared in defiant terms, "This isn't happening. This is not going to happen." Within a half hour we had secured a police car with a female officer. She wrapped the child in a heavy blanket and then put her into the back seat of the squad car. Fred and I followed as they moved through traffic on the way to the Department of Public Welfare, Gary office. Once there, things continued to move quickly. Emergency custody was secured and with Fred's assistance we got temporary placement at the Mayflower Home for Girls.

We left the girl with DPW authorities and got into our car. Fred said, "We have just one more thing to do before we get to the Mayflower Home. Wait for me as I run into this Sears department store." He came out with a fairly good sized bag.

"Fred, what's in the bag?"

"I have girls this age. They don't sleep well unless they can wrap their arms around a nice soft stuffed doll."

The Mayflower Home became a permanent placement. Mrs. King in the high school book store became the unofficial surrogate mother. Time moved on, as it always does, and newly neglected and abused children became our focus.

Some ten years later, I was teaching a college course to Chicago police officers—Psychology For Law Enforcement Officers. After class, a young officer stopped me and said, "Dr. Golarz, my wife is a new cop like me. She works the inner city here in Chicago with mostly neglected kids. She wanted me to ask you if you remember Marble Street." I said, "Sure I do."

He replied with a smile. "Well, she wanted you and Mr. Fred to know that she still has that nice soft stuffed doll."

"Close to the Blessed Virgin's Altar"

I went to a small college in East Chicago. The registration desk was near the front door. Any registration conversations you had would, consequently, not be private. So, when Michael entered, donned in a three piece olive green wool suit and bowler hat, there would be no confidentiality. He had come to enroll. Eventually, the clerk (Kathy) assisting his enrollment asked his preferred course of study. He laid his bowler hat on the counter and replied, "I'm here to initiate a Ph.D. program." The dean came over and said, "Son, this college offers only a bachelors degree program." At which Michael responded, "Well, then I assume you can get me started." We had a new freshman classmate.

Michael lived alone in an upscale rental apartment near our college. His payment in full for his college fall semester was no fluke. He always had money. Further, his olive green suit was only one of many elegant outfits. Despite his idiosyncrasies, we liked him. There was not a matched pair of human beings in our motley class. We each had our significant individualized transgressions. So he fit in. We came to like him so much that he was given the nickname "Duke." In those days when you were given a nickname you were "in."

Duke was a quiet guy who seemed to prefer being alone. Tom Sertich (Bull), one of our South Chicago classmates would have none of that and would drag Duke to places he didn't really want to go. Bull wasn't a guy you could resist. On Sundays when we played pick-up football games at Kosciuszko Park, Bull would often bring Duke. Duke never played but somehow he seemed to like being there. Only once did he even touch the ball. An out of bounds punt came right at him and he caught it. He seemed really surprised and pleased. We cheered. It was as if he had never caught a football before. At season's end Bull bought little three-inch high trophies at Woolworths. Everyone got one, including Duke.

Winter break, just after Christmas, Bull came to my house. He struggled to get it out. Duke had committed suicide. It was the foul odor in the hallway that prompted the police to go into his room. They found him lying on his bed decked out in his olive suit. It was some kind of overdose but he left no note. In his right hand he held his little three-inch high trophy.

There was no funeral. Someone from Boston claimed his body. The next week Bull went to the police department. A police officer, who was a friend of his, gave him the little trophy. In our first class after winter break we couldn't get past Duke's empty chair. Further, we hadn't yet spoken to one another about our deepest pain—the pain you feel when a loved one commits suicide. Should we have known?

All twenty-five of us left our books in class and walked the three blocks to Assumption church. Bull found the pastor and asked if he had a nice place for a little trophy.

Father said, "Was it Duke's?"

Bull nodded.

Father smiled and then said, "You know Duke never knew his own mother and though he was not Catholic he liked to come here and sit in the first pew, close to the Blessed Virgin's altar. How about if we put his trophy there?"

We knelt and prayed together near that altar, leaving one center empty seat. We sat silently in the caring presence of God until only the red vigil light and little votive candles gave soft light to the comforting and darkening church.

The glow of the candles performed a gentle and quiet dance on the front of the little trophy for all of us to see. If only we would have known. If only we would have known.

Joshua

My grandmother, (Busia) lived in an old neighborhood. The same neighborhood I grew up in. Her house was just down from the coal yard. The back of her house faced the alleyway that had on its far side a row of old unpainted and rotting clapboard garages and the back of Kot's bar.

It was a wintry, early December day when I stopped to have lunch with her. I was the novice director of a criminal justice delinquency intervention project. Much of the project focused upon my old neighborhood, known for its serious problem with juvenile delinquency.

I could see through the kitchen window two boys about ages 12 or 13 foraging for food in the alleyway garbage cans. I slipped on my coat and went out. They ran. They ended up hiding in a dark space between two old structures. I knew this hiding place, so it didn't take long to trap them. As I approached, the smaller of the two drew a handmade knife. I could have taken the knife but decided to talk them down. It took half-an-hour to convince them that my grandmother's warm kitchen, bowl of chicken soup, and homemade bread was a much better place than this cold dark refuge.

Busia had them wash, and then she sat them down in her kitchen near the potbellied stove. After a prayer, the homemade chicken soup and bread were attacked. The boys didn't look up or speak for the next 20 minutes. The smaller boy, who I found out was Joshua, finally looked up at Busia with a warm, relaxed, and deep smile-not a smile that I would ever forget.

We lost contact with the boys over that winter.

In early February I got word that the bigger boy, Noah had been hit by a car and was killed as he was running out of a neighborhood alley. We searched for Joshua for months but could not find him. Finally, I got a call from probation officer Sullivan in Judge Mazur's Juvenile court. "Ray, we think we found your kid. DPW is bringing him into court. Judge thought you might like to be here."

When I got there, Judge Mazur was placing him at the Crown Point juvenile detention facility pending placement to Hoosier Boys Town.

He then said to me, "Ray, would you like to take him over there?"

I responded, "Would love to, your Honor."

As we settled into my car, Joshua looked up at me and said,

"Mr. Ray, could we stop at Busia's house first for some chicken soup?'

I replied. "She already knows we're com'in, Joshua. She already knows we're com'in."

I visited Joshua fairly often at Hoosier Boy's Town. Finally he completed his studies, joined the military and was shipped off to Viet Nam. We soon lost contact. I never knew if he made it back. Somewhere in the coward section of my heart I didn't want to know. I didn't want to know that he hadn't. I just wanted to remember that warm and deep smile looking up from his chicken soup.

Then one day, as I was leaving the building after teaching my class, I was approached by a young, very handsome, uniformed Marine whom I didn't recognize. He looked into my eyes, smiled and said, "Mr. Ray, Busia still make that great chicken soup?" I yelled out "Joshua."

Then I grabbed him as he grabbed me. We held on for a long time. That night we sat at a table we had sat at before. We laughed, teared, and thanked God for the joy of one another.

Treasure God's Farmers

T he name that we affectionately called her was "Busia," the Polish
word for grandmother. On her acre property was a magnificent
apple tree planted at the height of the Great Depression in 1935. Each
summer it would bear wonderful fruit. Pies, canned apples, and apple
butter came from that fruit.

I can remember seeing her angry only once. It happened on a warm,
mid-summer day near the side of the house where that apple tree grew.
My brother Joe and I had gotten into an apple-throwing war with
neighborhood kids. The warring weaponry was apples that had fallen
to the ground. When Busia saw us, she rushed into the yard. She was
livid. It was an anger that we had never seen before. The warring enemy
ran and we were alone with her. As she pointed her finger at us, shaking
it repeatedly, we could see that her anger had brought her to tears.
Our immediate assumption was that we had provoked her wrath as a
consequence of fighting. We were wrong. Through her broken English
we began to understand something very different. We, her grandsons,
had been abusing a gift of precious food that God in his goodness
had given to her and her family. She was ashamed and disgraced. Still

sobbing, she picked up the battered apples lying on the ground, brushed off the dirt and gently placed them into her apron. She left us there feeling a shame we had never before felt.

Every year I had watched her faithfully plant and tend her garden and her fruit trees. I had even assisted her with the plants, pulling the weeds and hoeing the soil. But until we had seen her express such anger, neither I nor my brother Joe had understood what this all meant to her. This growing, nurturing, and eventual harvesting was not just a way of life; it was a daily communion with her God. Each plant and each tree was an act of faith that would bring a response in the form of a harvest—a response promised to an old peasant woman who understood and cherished this bond.

The next spring as my brother and I helped her plant her garden, we saw her do things that we had never before noticed. She spoke quietly to the seeds and the new sprouts. She tended to the soil around them ever so gently, noticing where additional soil might be needed or pressed more firmly. As weeks went by and we moved with her along the rows of plants, we could see that she knew each one, even anticipating what their needs might be. We were seeing things that we had not been previously aware of.

In the late summer and fall, the harvesting of her trees and plants was done in the manner of one accepting gifts from a gift-giver you are very fond of. During those times, in quiet evenings, she often hummed the tunes I believe she carried to this land from the old country. They were probably melodies she had learned as a child while assisting with the harvestings or as she walked through meadows tending the animals.

I have not, since my time with Busia, spent my life with farmers. As I grow older, I wish I had. I'm not sure that any of us should ever get too far from the soil or from those who spend their lives there and bring forth its gifts. They seem to have learned better how to live their lives in a simpler, more harmonious way with their God and His creation.

The Starfish

I finished a keynote address in Phoenix when a young teacher came to the stage and handed me a gold colored lapel starfish pin. She said, "Please wear it. You made a difference today."

I was taken with this special gesture and asked friends what the starfish pin symbolized. Dr. Dave Hrach, Superintendent of Tombstone, explained, "Ray, it comes from a story written by Loren Eisley. It goes like this."

"One day a man was walking along the beach when he noticed a boy picking something up and gently throwing it into the ocean. Approaching the boy, he asked, 'What are you doing?' The youth replied, 'Throwing starfish back into the ocean. The surf is up and the tide is going out. If I don't throw them back, they'll die.' 'Son,' the man said, 'don't you realize there are miles and miles of beach and thousands of starfish? You can't possibly make a difference!' After listening politely, the boy bent down, picked up another starfish, and threw it back into the surf. Then, smiling at the man, he said, 'It made a difference for that one.'"

When I got back home, with the school board's approval we ordered enough pins for all of our staff. A special note went with the starfish pin telling the starfish story and then asking them to wear the pin because they daily made a difference.

The starfish were an immediate hit. Teachers, secretaries, and custodians seeing each other's pins in the hardware store or on the street were giving each other a high five.

Sometime later I was concluding a meeting with principals. As they were leaving, John a high school principal asked if we had any more of the starfish pins. Mike, one of his assistant principals had given his pin to an aide who had not received one. I advised John that we had ordered more but at the moment we had none. He seemed disappointed, so I said, "Here, John, take mine, but don't tell Mike where it came from otherwise he might not want to take it." John resisted but I made him take it.

Several weeks later I got a phone call from John. "Ray, we have an emergency. My assistant principal Mike had a heart attack between classes in a hallway. No one found him lying there until change of classes. He's being helicoptered to Indianapolis." I hung up then informed board members. At the hospital Mike was declared critical.

The next weeks were stressful, but eventually Mike got home. Soon afterwards we had high school graduation. Mike's doctors encouraged him not to come. But, really—you know Mike.

In the auditorium, Mike came running up to me and with his forever big smile said.

"Dr. Golarz do you know why I'm alive?" I was completely disarmed. He then said, "The starfish."

I'm sure I looked puzzled so he continued, "When I lay in the hallway, unable to move, my head was turned to my coat lapel, the sun was shining through the skylight onto my starfish pin. It was sparkling and glowing at me. I knew then that I had something yet to do and so I hung on."

He continued to smile, but I was too choked up to respond. We went on stage and handed out diplomas.

I never told Mike that he wore my starfish pin.

I never understood why I gave my starfish pin to John for Mike but I have come to recognize in my older age that God will forever nudge us to do such things.

An Island of Civility

S adly, today most Americans have been influenced to believe that the primary purpose of education is to cause students to become more cognitively proficient in the studies of mathematics, technology and science. Measuring the success or failure of this endeavor is most often assessed by objective testing. Ultimately one's value as a person is relegated to a set of these test scores.

Some years ago in response to this change that was moving schooling further away from cherished outcomes such as truthfulness, kindness, empathy, and decency, I met with a group of sixty administrators representing elementary, middle and high schools. Could we reverse the trend in our own schools? Could we nudge our school community back to seeing the importance of honorable human qualities? Could we create an island of civility?

We came up with a plan. We would focus the school district on the human qualities we most respected, qualities that if instilled in all of us would change a world needing such change. Our plan was simple. First, we would advise our communities that the development and recognition of such personal qualities was a major purpose of schools. Second, during the next several months we would ask each school community to identify two teachers, two non-certified staff, and seven students from their school who had exhibited in a remarkable way such personal qualities. Finally, at a public school board meeting in the spring, we would recognize and honor all of these persons who had been selected.

Within a short time after implementing the plan, unanticipated changes seemed to occur throughout the district. Many expressed feeling a subtle, quiet peace. Along with that feeling of peace other significant changes occurred. There were fewer suspensions for fights, the dropout rate went down, and, most notably, a number of teachers who were planning retirement decided to stay.

At a board meeting the following spring, each of those identified received a certificate of honor with their name inscribed and signed by school leaders. The awards were handed to each of them by their own parent or spouse. A reception followed.

I left the district sometime after that, but was advised by colleagues that the practice we had initiated continued for the next several years. It was distressing to hear that it ended. I remember being sad at the thought that a very special practice was gone and, I assumed, quite probably would be forgotten.

Some 25 years later, I was scheduled to speak at a conference on Bainbridge Island near Seattle. When I arrived, my host said that a very prosperous business community leader, known for his practices of treating his employees with honor and dignity, asked if he could attend my presentation. I had, of course, no objection. After my presentation we met. I was stunned to learn that he was born and raised in my own home community. He explained excitedly his daily practices of finding ways to dignify his 1,500 employees. He spoke of the culture he was attempting to create and of the awards being given to employees who manifested kindness and generosity.

I was immediately reminded of the practice I had been a part of so many years earlier. I told him of it. He smiled and said, "I know, Dr. Golarz. You see, I was a seventh grader at Lafayette School in those days. My mom was sick and couldn't be at the school board meeting that night, so you handed me my award."

"I shot an arrow into the air
It fell to earth, I knew not where;"
Longfellow

The Real World

With my master's degree in hand from Indiana University I got a job. I had already taught middle and high school for several years, so I was a perfect fit for the school district's new federally-funded delinquency prevention effort. They wanted staff that had some teaching experience.

My first day on the job, at 7:45 A.M., I met my mentor at a house in a heavily industrialized part of town. The house was one of the few remaining in an area of condemned houses being razed as a part of a redevelopment effort. I pulled up, and Andy Hiduke was already there waiting for me.

"Have a hard time finding it, kid?"

"No, not really. Just didn't realize there were still homes in this area."

"Won't be for long, kid. Won't be for long."

I followed him up the broken concrete sidewalk to the house. Andy was an old salt—reminded me of some Navy petty officers I had served under, the kind of guys you could work with for thirty years and still not tap all that they knew or could teach you. He had been doing police and court work for years, during which time he had been Chief Probation Officer for the Lake County Juvenile Court. He was a crusty tough veteran who clearly knew his way around the darker parts of the community.

As we cautiously continued down the dangerously cracked and broken sidewalk to the house, Andy turned to me and said,

"These are poor but proud people, Ray. She will, in her way, have cleaned the house for our coming, but it smells so bad in there that you won't notice her efforts. She may also have gotten a little coffee from somewhere and made some for us. If she offers, accept. She has little else. Their last name is White. They have fourteen children. Nine still live in the house. The two oldest sons are doing time at the State Penitentiary for armed robbery. The whereabouts of the two older girls and an older son, all dropouts, are unknown." As we approached the front door it was opened to us by a barefoot and scantily dressed boy who appeared to be about four years old.

"Hello, Mr. Andy."

Andy replied, "Samuel."

Then we heard from within the house, "Mr. Andy, you just come in here and bring your friend too."

We walked through the living room and into the kitchen. There we found Mrs. White. She was an extremely large woman. I knew from earlier conversations with Andy that she was in her mid-forties, but she appeared much older. Life had been hard. "Would you want some coffee?" We accepted and sat. One of the several young girls near the kitchen served us. Andy then advised Mrs. White that I would be working with her and her family. At this she seemed quite distressed.

She turned to me and asked, "Will you remember to bring us a food order if we need one?" I smiled and replied, "Yes, ma'am. I'll remember, I promise."

She smiled back and seemed to relax. As Andy took over the conversation, out of the corner of my eye I watched a large roach working its way along the kitchen door frame toward a fairly sizable hole in the ceiling. While I continued to glance around from where I sat between the kitchen and living room, I could see in the living room stacks and stacks of disorganized clothing, blankets, bedding, and badly torn furniture and mattresses. In and amongst these stacks and piles were small half-naked children playing everywhere.

I turned back to the table at the very moment that a large roach dropped from the large hole in the ceiling. It landed no more than an inch from Andy's hand that was gripping his coffee mug. He did not move. He didn't in any way act startled. He did nothing to shame or humiliate this poor woman who, though she had little, was attempting to give us her best. He was the noblest of gracious guests and I felt God's caring presence seated next to him.

As we left the White's house that day and went to our cars, I looked up and said a little "thank you." I had come to this job with my new university degree, but I had been taught more on my first day, in an old run-down house, by a seasoned mentor than I ever could have imagined. Andy looked back as he entered his car and with just a trace of a smile on his face, he slowly nodded and with a knowing look said,

"Welcome to the real world, kid. Welcome to the real world."

Edge of Real

~

Joshua

It was 1870 in the Upper Midwest of the USA. Monks came to build their monastery. The surrounding grounds were perfect for gardening and the planting of fruit trees. A clear river at the base of the largest hill would provide water. Soon the harvests were plentiful but laborers few. So the monks encouraged young men of their faith to enter the monastery and become brothers.

Joshua arrived in twilight. "I would like to become a brother." It was clear that Joshua was lacking both in manner and mind. He was nevertheless accepted provisionally. The following late afternoon he was given the task of securing two buckets of evening drinking water from the river below. As Joshua climbed the hill with the two full wooden buckets, he tripped and fell. The buckets rolled and bounced down the hill, hitting large trees and breaking into many pieces. He knelt, wept and prayed at the grotto of the Virgin Mary. Nonetheless, he was advised that he would need to leave. In the afternoon of the next day two young monks were assigned to retrieve the broken buckets. As they were bringing back the broken pieces, they passed the Virgin's grotto at the top of the hill and found two full wooden buckets. This was mysterious since the monastery had only two wooden buckets.

Inexplicably, monasteries in Brussels and Amsterdam reported of an unassuming and unskilled gentle young man named Joshua seeking work with them on that very same day. Neither accepted him.

In the years that followed, the simple, both in manner and mind, were never again turned away.

Jeremiah

Jeremiah was questioning his vocation. He thought that an evening walk might comfort him. As he walked the older part of the monastery grounds and prayed, he encountered an old monk at the edge of a red brick path. As he approached the old Monk he felt a chill run throughout his body. Somehow in that moment he was aware of the caring presence of God.

"Forgive me, Father, I do not know you."

"I'm Father Sebastian. "

'" Father, can we talk?"

They sat and talked until dawn. That morning, more comfortable about his vocation, Jeremiah went to the rector's office. "Father, I was very confused and fearful of losing my vocation. But I had a long talk with Father Sebastian last night, and everything is now so clear."

"Father Sebastian?"

"Yes Father, that's his picture on the wall behind you."

"Jeremiah, that is a picture of Father Sebastian, but he died in 1860 over 100 years ago and is buried in our monastery cemetery at the edge of the red brick path."

Friar Dominic

A soft banging could be heard in the basement of the four-story monastery. Father Caspian, the rector, sent for a plumber. The plumber worked on the furnace and the banging stopped. Weeks later as the monks were at Vespers the banging began again—now more intense. The plumber was sent for and came again. He could find nothing wrong. The pounding in the basement continued. A second plumber came. After an extensive inspection, he advised the rector that whatever was causing the pounding was not coming from the furnace or pipes.

Within a week, just before dawn, the pounding became deafening and was clearly coming from the basement's west wall. The elderly and wise Friar Dominic was called upon. He advised, "Begin saying masses for the dead." Subsequently, the pounding completely stopped. The masses continued.

Incidentally, the four-story monastery is easy to find. It has a charming garden cemetery for deceased monks that butts up against its west basement wall.

How far is the edge of real? How sure are we that the edge of real is far away at all? Are there realms of God's presence and love that we simply don't understand?

The Christmas Purse

During the Great Depression, many women in the poverty communities of America did house work for the families of means. The homes of these wealthy families were in more affluent neighborhoods. Most of these affluent neighborhoods were some distance from the neighborhoods of the poor. To get to work, a woman had normally only two options: take a bus that would cost her five cents each way, or walk. The option that was always taken, despite the weather or how well she felt, was to walk. Walking saved her a dime and a dime was the price of a loaf of bread. The shortest path of that walk, regardless as to where she lived in this country, was normally along a railroad track. Once the track approached the affluent neighborhood she would leave the tracks and head to the house where she was employed.

House cleaning work was sought after. Although it paid only about 15 cents per hour, an average week's pay of approximately $3.00 paid for a family's weekly food and sometimes also a pair of shoes. Most men at that time were unemployed, so the house work money of the mother and daughters, if a household had a daughter who could also work, provided the primary and often only source of family income.

The date was Friday, December 21, 1934, three days before the Polish Wigilia (the Christmas Eve traditional meal). It was 6:15 P.M. and the temperature outside was 12 degrees above zero. It was also quite windy. Ma Jabrewski was very late coming home from work. Pa and her two older sons Walt and Lefty were getting very nervous. On Fridays she was normally home by 3:30 P.M. Lefty was getting dressed to go out and look for her.

At that moment there was heavy pounding at the back door. The door then swung open and Ma, tripping on the top entryway stair, fell into the kitchen with a horrendous thud. As she fell, Lefty and Walt were immediately at her side. Pa and their younger sister Anne came rushing from the living room. As they lifted her, they could feel that her hands were icy cold and bleeding. Further, blood was running down the front of both legs from her knees that were badly scratched, bruised, and dirty. Somewhere she had lost her head scarf, and her hair was in a total state of disarray, her face beet-red and dirty. She looked up, crying. At that moment, Pa gently lifted her into his arms and said quietly and gently, "Mary, Mary." He held her there for a while in the kitchen and then carried her to a comfortable place in the living room.

When she finally calmed a bit, they asked her what had happened. She explained that on the way home she lost her change purse—the little black one with blue and green flowers. The change purse contained this week's wages of $3.70, her Christmas Eve meal money. She said she knew she had it when she was on the tracks because just before then she had used her handkerchief to wipe her face and the change purse was in her coat pocket. When she was still on the tracks, but nearer home, she felt for it and it was gone. She said then that she searched and searched, often on her hands and knees, but she couldn't find it. Then it was getting dark so she came home to get a flashlight. She then wept.

Lefty, visibly shaken, looked at his mother and said, "Don't worry, Ma, we'll find it." Then to Walt he asked, "Ready?"

Walt responded, "Let's go. Get a flashlight and a lantern."

As they walked towards the tracks, Lefty and Walt stopped at

Kal's house to let him know that they wouldn't be home and could, therefore, not get together with him as planned. They also told him what they were about and then proceeded to the tracks where it was cold, quite windy, and dark. They started with the location where Ma told them she first felt the purse gone. Then slowly, with their flashlight and lantern turned on, they walked her route northwest to where she would have begun to walk the tracks. They had walked slowly but had found nothing.

It was now near 8:30 P.M., the wind was picking up and the temperature was dropping. They turned back and began to retrace their steps—now a little less confident.

As they walked back, they could see that they were approaching several lights in the distance. As they got closer, they could hear faint talking from the location of the lights that now seemed to be moving toward them. They then heard a shout from a voice they immediately recognized to be Kal Borbely's.

Kal spoke, "Hey, what you two guys doin' on the tracks? Looking to steal coal?"

Lefty responds, "That you, Kal?"

Kal replies, "Who the hell do you think it is—an early Santa Claus with a bunch of elves?"

By this time, they were coming upon the group of nine or ten of their semi-pro football teammates. Walt yelled out, "What are all you guys doin' out here?"

Johnny Gorski jokingly responded, "We heard that the last engineer who came racing through here shook his train and left coins all over the damn tracks. Hi ya, Walt."

Walt said, "Thanks for coming, Johnny."

Johnny replied, "Hey, bunch of us were just sittin' around a warm fire at Wusic's gas station just gettin' fat and needing a brisk walk outdoors when Kal told us about your Ma's purse. So, what would you like us to do?"

Walt said, "Well, how about if we all stay together, spread out along the track, and slowly walk the whole distance Ma walked back and forth until we find it."

Gorski agreed, "That's as good a plan as any. Let's do it."

For the next three hours on that cold and windy night, the teammates searched along the track for the little flowered purse. Back and forth. Back and forth. Back and forth. It was now nearing midnight when behind Walt and Lefty, who were in the lead along the track, Gorski exclaimed, "We found it."

Walt and Lefty turned and raced back to where Gorski was standing. Everyone gathered around as Gorski, with both of his hands overlapped and cupped together, held an overflowing pile of coins, mostly dimes, nickels, and pennies. As Lefty and Walt stood dumbstruck, looking at his hands with this pile of money, Johnny Gorski said, "It's $3.61. Somewhere nine cents fell out of your Ma's purse."

Walt, shaking his head slowly looked up into Johnny's eyes and said, "Johnny, we can't take this money from you guys."

Johnny simply said, "We aren't givin' it to you and Lefty. It's for a little old Polish lady, sitting and praying in your living room that her sons are gonna find her purse with her Christmas meal money like they promised they would."

Lefty just stood there, his arms down at his sides. He was psychologically defenseless. As he looked at Johnny and the others, it was clear that he was having trouble holding it together. His friends and teammates were giving to them every penny they had. He took a deep breath, swallowed, and shaking his head, just looked at his friends, this band of teammates. Though he tried, he wasn't successful in holding back the tears.

At close to 1:00 A.M. that morning, Ma got her $3.61. She knew it wasn't hers because she had three dollar bills, two quarters, and two dimes in her change purse. But they made her take it.

She was never told who specifically was out there that night, but from that day, whenever any of her sons' teammates were in the house, there was a small pot of coffee on the stove.

The little change purse was never found

Catherine

World War II had ended. Church bells rang and there was happiness everywhere. My grandmother (Busia) sent me down the alley to the butcher shop for three slices of baloney. Tonight for dinner we would celebrate. I was just a kid, so I didn't understand rationing, nor how poor we were.

That fall I started school at Saint Mary's, five blocks down the street. The building had been constructed in the 1870s. It had clapboard siding with very large windows and no insulation. In winter you prayed that your seat was near the potbellied stove up front. In addition to the four classrooms there was a large storage room upstairs that was seldom used except when the nuns took the seventh grade girls up there for a talk. Fifty yards from the school building on the edge of the gravel playground were the outhouses. You had to walk five feet down on the concrete stairs to get to the toilets and urinals. You ventured there only if you really needed to because the smell was nauseating, and it was not uncommon for a big kid to take any money you had.

Late fall during fourth grade I met Catherine. I had seen her in class but we had never spoken. There were four girls beating her up on the edge of the playground as she was trying to walk home. They were pulling her hair, kicking and spitting on her. She was crying, helpless, and on her knees. I yelled and shooed them away. They screamed out that they would get her again. She then raised her head while tears streamed down her dirty face. I said "Why?" She just shrugged her shoulders and wept. She resisted my walking her home, but I was hearing none of that. I wiped off her dirty face and found her books. "Where's your coat?" "I'm Ok." I wrapped my coat around her. It was bitterly cold that afternoon. She said very little as we walked.

When we got to her house—a one room apartment at the end of eight other one room apartments, she opened the door. As I glanced in, even though I was a child, I recognized the gloomy, frightening look of abject poverty, and the memory of that glance still haunts me.

I told Busia everything. She listened and seemed to understand more profoundly than me. I learned later that Catherine's dad was killed at Iwo Jima and that her mom drank a lot. Soon Busia contacted some neighborhood ladies, including Mrs. Jeblonowski from Kenwood Street, a seamstress. Together they made a coat, two dresses, and bought her new socks and shoes.

On December 23rd, two days before Christmas, Busia and Mrs. Jeblonowski had Catherine and her mother over. They took Catherine into Busia's bedroom and dressed her up. When they came out I'm sure I had never seen a bigger smile on a little girl's face. Her mom just cried.

I often walked Catherine home from school after that, especially when it appeared that someone might try to hurt her. It got around that I was watching out for her.

As I reflect on those years, I recognize now that we didn't have much, but knowing Catherine made me understand that we weren't really poor.

Someday I hope that the memory of my childhood glance of a very empty, depressing dark room fades away, but if it means that I must also forget the biggest Christmas smile I have ever seen on a little girl's face, I'll keep the memories.

Who Can Judge

At age 12, after school, Bobby and I would meet at the corner of Fields and Howard, throw our coats to the ground, and fight. Thirty or so kids would watch. Sometimes Bobby would win, sometimes I would. Afterwards, we would head to the coal yard, find a high pile to sit on, talk and have a smoke. I learned a lot about Bobby those late afternoons—no dad, an alcoholic mom, and a grandfather who liked to use him as a punching bag. I had so much more, yet for all of our differences we were much alike—a couple of street kids who liked to fight and liked one another. Our neighborhood had lots of little stores, no end of bars, and only a few churches—mostly Catholic. Stealing was commonplace and many older guys were armed.

It was predictable that we would eventually plan something illegal. As fate would have it, the night it was planned for, my dad insisted that I drive with him to the north side of town to pick up a load of lumber. Bobby and three others were caught, arrested, and sent to boy's school. While at boy's school, Bobby got into very serious trouble and ended up in an adult security prison. We lost contact.

Eventually, I became a high school teacher. Our school decided to sponsor a program of delinquency prevention. Penitentiary prisoners in shackles would present an auditorium session. That morning I sat with my class in the auditorium. The sound of the prisoners' shackles as they walked to the stage was eerie and frightening. The auditorium became deathly quiet except for that sound. The last prisoner hit me on the shoulder as he passed. I was stunned. As they presented, I strained to see if I could recognize him. Eventually, they finished and began their walk back. As the last prisoner got closer, I experienced a cold, overwhelming chill. It was Bobby—older, thinner and drawn—but Bobby. Guards gave us a moment in the back of the auditorium. Bobby asked about my Dad and brother Joe. I could think of nothing except that I wanted to free him and run until we could hide together, safe in the coal yard. He sensed it and said, "Ray, it's OK. For some reason we are both where we need to be. Don't try to figure out why." He would forever be my friend.

The next day Juan Domingo, one of the toughest delinquent kids I have ever known, came to my classroom. "I saw you talkin' to the con in the auditorium yesterday. How do I get in touch with him?" I told him. He nodded and then he left.

Some twenty years later, I was sitting in my administrative office. My secretary Phyllis came in, "Dr. Golarz, you have a call holding from a Captain Domingo of narcotics operations, Chicago Police." Somewhat perplexed, yet somehow knowing, I answered and heard. "Mr. Golarz?" "Yes." "Bobby passed away in prison last night. He made me promise that if it ever happened, to make sure you knew right away." "Thanks, Captain. Thank you for calling." "No problem, I owed him much. I'm sure you, like no one else would understand that." He then hung up.

I called my Dad and brother Joe. I asked them to meet me at old Saint Mary's Church to say a prayer for a street kid from the neighborhood. On my way to church, I stopped momentarily at the corner of Fields and Howard. I rolled my window down. Through the heavy falling snow, my mind's eye could almost make them out—two street kids who liked to fight and who loved one another.

When I got to the church, there was significant snow accumulating on Joe's and Dad's cars. After parking I walked the short distance to the church. I opened the heavy church door. The red vigil light and little votive candles gave a soft glow to the inside of the dark church. I could see them both up front in the first pew. All around me I could feel an intense caring presence. I went up and knelt with them.

Then dad quietly said, "Polish or English, kid?" I replied. "I think he'd like Polish Pa….I'm sure he would." Then with the sign of the cross we began. "Wimio Ojca I Syna I Ducha…." Three Polish East Hammond street kids answering the request of another Polish street kid who was now in a better place.

Who can judge the better life lived?

When God Takes the Young

I t was a rather chilly, overcast, late October day. The waves on the lake in front of the seminary were beginning to show white caps as the wind coming across the lake intensified. But we were 14 years old and intent on taking out one of the seminary row boats. We zipped up our jackets, pulled down our wool caps, untied the craft from the dock, and went forth.

Both oar locks were broken, so we had to row canoe style. The wind continued in its intensity, blowing straight at us as it came across the lake. We got out about 50 yards from shore when it became very clear that we needed to head back.

It was at that moment that we could hear through the howling wind pleas for help coming from across the water to our right. Through the wind and rain we could see another boat capsized some 150 yards away. Clearly it was farther from shore than we were. We could see someone clinging to the overturned boat. The screams for help continued, and with haste, we attempted to row in that direction, but now the side of our boat was taking the brunt of the storm. We kept rowing, but the storm was driving us to the break wall. Finally, we hit the breakwall, left our boat, and ran the 100 yards to the shore nearest the capsized boat.

When we got there, several priests and a handful of seminarians had been gathering and were engaged in rescue efforts. Three of our fellow seminarians had been in that boat. Only one could be seen clinging to the overturned craft. Two of the younger priests had stripped and were diving.

Eventually two of our classmates, still fully clothed, were dragged from the lake in front of us on the shore. The agony of that moment can't ever be erased from the minds of those of us who were there. Fr. John, weeping and on his knees between their bodies, led us in prayer on that beach as more and more of our classmates arrived from different seminary locations.

As with any school there are the athletes, the jokesters, the quiet ones, the scholars, and the ones we all want to be near because they so remind us of what Christ must have been like. Such were Tom and Rich. We all knew that God had marked them in a special way.

I don't remember any of us eating dinner that late afternoon or evening. We all simply gathered in the chapel. I'm sure someone led us in prayer but I don't remember who. I just remember how the vigil light seemed to get brighter as the church darkened.

That night my friend John and I met in the chapel at 3:00 A. M., to say a special private prayer. When we arrived we found that it was not possible to find an empty pew or seat. All 350 of us would sit that night in the caring presence of our God. With Him we would weep. This sort of spontaneous sensitivity went on for months. The seminary got to be a little quieter, and we a little more reflective, a little kinder, and maybe, just maybe, a little holier.

We had taken from us two who we knew were the best of us. Their absence left a beckoning hole, a lonely spot that we all felt. It didn't take long for us to see the need to fill that hole with our own good will. Possibly we hoped to somehow give meaning to our lives through the gift of their very beautiful and short ones—lives that we all knew would have been special.

Is this possibly why so many good die so young? To give us the motivation to do good in their absence—the good we know they would have done?

I don't know, but I hope so.

A Christmas Card

H is name was Tom. He was a student in my government class. He possessed a provocative depth of inquiry not found in most his age.

On a cold, Friday afternoon in February we were studying the disparity of wealth existing among nations. I could see that Tom was thinking intensely about the topic, yet he did not participate—he said nothing. Finally, I said to him, "Tom, what are you thinking?" He looked up and somewhat apologetically said, "I'd rather not say." I gently persisted. Tom answered. His response was neither adversarial nor challenging. He simply said, "Mr. Golarz, there's no morality in the world." His response was clearly not cognitive, but rather a response that seemed to come from someplace deep inside of his soul. Had it been cognitive, I would have debated. But his response was clearly more in the manner of a core value. So I simply said, "Tom, I disagree." Soon class was over. I sat in the faculty lounge lamenting that I did not have the skill to dissuade him of his position. I felt, as teachers often do, that I had failed him. Where was the magic of wisdom?

Several weeks later there was a scheduled exam. Three students, including Tom, missed the exam. Tom's absence was for a reason that did not require my permitting a makeup exam. Several days later, as students were leaving class, I asked Tom to wait. When we were alone, I said, "Tom I'll be in the building late tomorrow. If you would like to come by and make up the exam, I'll be here." He looked surprised and said, "That's awfully nice of you, Mr. Golarz." The next thing I said I hadn't planned. It just came out of me almost as a gift to me from God—the the kind of gift teachers often get. I said, "Tom it's simply the moral thing to do." He looked stunned. I continued, "Will you be there?" After a long moment, he said quietly and slowly, "Yes, sir. I'll be there."

Tom took his exam. We never discussed my comment. Several months later he graduated. Six months after graduation, I received a phone call near midnight, "Mr. Golarz, this is Tom. Do you think we could have coffee and talk?" A half hour later we met at George's Diner. We drank coffee and talked all night. At 7 a.m., I shaved in the faculty lounge and went to teach. (Those were the days.) We met again and talked most of the night. Soon thereafter we lost contact. I learned years later that he was wounded severely in military action and decorated for valor. I had heard no more of Tom until recently. My wife Marion gets Christmas cards. One evening while reading the cards she asked, "Who's Tom?" It had been so many years I had forgotten, but it was from the Tom I had taught so long ago.

He wrote, "This Christmas thank-you note is long overdue. I'm an engineer in California now, and many evenings I coach basketball for wheelchair-handicapped kids. One of my kids who also struggles emotionally and wanted to give up recently asked me, "Coach, why do you give me so many chances?"

I wanted to tell him that it was "simply the moral thing to do," but I'm not sure he would have understood. I know, however, that you will understand. So thanks, Mr. Golarz, thanks for George's Diner and the all-nighters. I treasure that card. Wouldn't you?

Dumas, Chopin, and Pride

It was a very cold, windy, late November Saturday morning with traces of snow in the air as I was completing my drive to Dumas Elementary School on Chicago's South Side. The neighborhood had the look of post WWII Germany with only a sprinkling of very old houses, most abandoned—some simply in disrepair. The few business establishments had iron grates on all of the windows and doors. The occasional oil-drum fires where heavily clothed men gathered in an attempt to keep warm were the only signs of human occupancy.

I continued to drive. Slowly there appeared a greater number of houses and businesses. Finally, I came upon a one-story brick school building. I pulled up and turned off my car. Almost immediately four fairly good sized men approached and surrounded my car. I was anxious. The largest leaned over close to my driver side window and asked, "Are you Dr. Golarz?" I nodded. In an authoritative tone he said, "Come with us. We're your body guards." In the building, Sylvia Peters, the principal, wrapped her arms around me and said, "Thanks for coming. Welcome to Dumas."

Some months earlier, I had agreed to keynote her school's Celebration of Learning. Sylvia introduced me to four sixth-grade students—three girls and a boy. She told me, "These children have won the honor of showing you around their school. They each led the entire school and community in the annual candle-light ceremony this year. Please go with them." I nodded and then the smallest of the three girls took my hand, looked up, smiled and said, "Dr. Golarz, do you enjoy Chopin?" I was completely taken aback, then responded, "Why, yes, I do." As we walked, the young man chimed in, "Chopin is the composer of the month. All of our language arts and our creative writings have him and his music as our central theme. Last month it was Schubert and next month Handel."

As we talked, we passed by classroom after classroom. Each classroom door was decorated with a collage of pictures and historical information which related to a particular composer. I had not expected to experience what I was being shown. Is this what our nation defines as dysfunctional? Then Sylvia explained that though the great composers' curricular design was of immense pride to her school, it was but one of the strategies designed to facilitate student capacity and their more extensive depth of knowing. She further told me that she had cajoled local businesses into donating violins, cellos, woodwinds, brass, and percussion instruments so that Dumas Elementary could have an orchestra—a meaningful connection to the composers her students were studying, and a touch of class to match the newly found dignity of her students and their community. Sixty years of educational research affirms that individual schools are the most effective units of improvement—never state legislatures. When will we ever learn!

As I drove away, the neighborhood seemed a little brighter. Most of Sylvia's students were still struggling to read at grade level, most were still hungry when they woke up each morning, and most would never experience a home with a father and a mother—many with neither parent. But they had a neighborhood public school that offered hope and provided pride.

As for me, I got a special gift that snowy November morning, for whenever I hear the music of Chopin, I picture the beautiful, proud face of a young African-American girl who captured my heart and said to me with a smile,

"Dr. Golarz, Do you enjoy Chopin?"

The Saw Sharpener

Most old country neighborhoods had a saw sharpener. My Grandfather (Dziadzia) was that craftsman. As with all artisans, his tools were trustworthy and simple. The real skills needed to do a fine job were, however, in the experienced feel of the hands and arms of the craftsman.

Joe and I, my sister Barbara, and an array of neighborhood kids always liked to watch him work. The wooden saw horse that securely held the saw being worked on was the centerpiece of the crafting endeavor. The many and various files used in his work were kept indoors in the basement. As he considered the work needed to sharpen a saw, he would first take that saw into the basement and then carefully choose the files he wanted and then come back outside to the wooden saw horse.

He seemed to most enjoy his work during the warmest part of summer afternoons. Perhaps in this manner he was less pained by his arthritis. He always donned an old baseball cap, wore a long-sleeved white undershirt, and tied a red bandana around his neck.

He would start out by placing his left foot on an elevated two-by-four of the saw horse. Then with the file placed properly in his hands, he would slowly move the file back and forth. Somewhat, like a golfer following through on his swing, he would lift the file off of the saw as he came to the end of a movement. Eventually, after many such passes, his entire body would flow in a wave-like motion—to and fro, to and fro. Finally, he would turn his attention to each tooth of the saw and then his technique would always be gentler and more relaxed, and the files used would be the smallest and most delicate.

He kept a pint of Seagram's in his right back pants pocket, and by the end of a long afternoon two or three saws would have experienced the master's touch and the pint would be no more. The children, quite probably sitting with God on the grass in front of him, would be mesmerized by the rhythmic, shrill, steel-on-steel symphony of sounds. He would talk to them as he worked and ask us to note the differences in the sounds as the files did their work with each tooth. As he worked, he would explain:

"The hard work that the saw did over time changed it. It has lost its harmony. The work of the files brings that harmony back. Listen to how the sound of the file and the sound of the saw are blending. When that sound becomes one and the scratch is no more, then the tooth of the saw is good. When all of the teeth have the sound of one, the saw is good. It is again in God's harmony. For the carpenter who brought to me his saw, work with the saw can once again become a work of joy.

With your own lives, you can sometimes lose the harmony God wanted for you. So find tools that will bring you back. Use them to repair yourself and bring back your harmony and joy."

He would then smile at us, pull his tobacco pouch out from his shirt pocket, roll one, light it, then lean back on his bench and exhale smoke slowly into the summer sky. In that same manner he slowly and intentionally breathed into our lives awareness and love of God's harmony and then patiently and lovingly exhaled it upon us.

All we had to do was to breathe it in.

A Captain on God's
First Team

Richard had watched his older brothers play in division one college football. He thus grew to love the sport. As a young child, Richard's development had been erratic. He did not speak until he was four. Then his first words came in full sentences. He could recall and recite full conversations. He could say the alphabet backwards and from memory recite full children's stories backwards, word for word. Yet from age two, loud noises really upset him and he often did not want to be touched. Social interactions and early schooling were tough. Kids seemed to sense his naiveté and vulnerability. He got picked on and humiliated a lot.

During eighth grade he decided to follow his dream. At 5:30 every morning, regardless of inclement weather, he would run along the railroad tracks near his house. Afternoons he would work with weights. He made the football team. He was neither the fastest, nor strongest, but no one tried harder. By his senior year he started on defense and achieved a degree of recognition.

At season's end, he was selected as an alternate to the state all-star football game, which meant that he could play if the selected player could not make it. That happened, so Richard got to go. The game turned out to be a four quarter smash mouth battle. Richard saw little playing time.

At game's end, the coach sought out Richard's parents. "Mr. and Mrs. Simpson, can we talk?" "Certainly, coach." He then said, "Last night our team visited a facility for handicapped children. Once in the facility, our team was introduced to a large group of the handicapped children. For a moment things became extremely awkward and silent.

Then, purposefully, one of our players gently nudged his teammates aside, crossed the space between the team and the children, got on the floor, and began playing with these handicapped children. Soon, with delight, the children were all around him—engaged, smiling, touching and hugging him. He then looked up and gestured to his teammates to come forth and join him on the floor. Many did and the awkwardness melted away. As long as I live I will not forget that splendid moment of big football players and the smaller handicapped children on the floor playing together. Needless to say, in that moment there was not an adult dry eye in the facility. It was magic.

The player who made this all happen, the player who crossed that floor without hesitation, was your son, Richard—a young man who clearly has a sensitivity and humanity that few possess."

The Simpsons were quite moved.

And then the coach went on. "It's no secret that this will be my last year coaching. I am quite ill. So I pray every day that when I go up there, God will allow me to coach His heavenly team. We all know He has one. And as much as I love these extraordinarily athletic players I have coached, I pray to have a team made up of Richards.

After Richard completes his long and productive life here on earth, and it is finally his time to come, I will look for him. You see, I'll need a defensive captain up there, and I will be holding that spot open for him."

Gunny Sacks of Pride

The weather prediction for the weekend of November 28th and 29th of 1936 was bitter cold and windy with a threat of heavy lake effect snow on Monday. Therefore, a coal run along the tracks was needed immediately. Whoever could help was being asked to meet at Wusik's gas station on Saturday evening about 6:00 P.M., dress warm, bring lots of gunny sacks, flashlights and lanterns, and be prepared for an all-nighter on the tracks. If snow did come on Monday, it would be impossible to find coal, so Saturday and Sunday nights would be coal runs that would hopefully result in great hauls.

At 6:00 p.m. Saturday, it was ten degrees with a light wind that made it feel like ten below. Many young men from the community had dressed heavily. As bad as the weather was outside it would only get worse. Therefore, no time to delay. They took off, heading for the southeast end of the coal run near Indianapolis Boulevard. They would then work their way back to Columbia Ave—three miles of track.

Others began trickling in, and by 7:15 P.M., there were twelve more guys dressed warm and ready to go. Sometime around 10:00 P.M., the first group came back looking half-frozen, but their sacks were full.

"How bad was it out there?"

"Really bitter!"

"When you guys get warmed up, Wusik's got a list of names for you to take these first loads of coal to. Kominski's have no coal at all, so two or three of you will need to build 'em a fire and get their furnace going. Oh, drink all of the coffee you want. Mr. Wleklinski and Mr. Guyeski came with a gift from the Polish National Alliance about 8:00 tonight, enough coffee to last us for two weeks if we're careful. They also gave us the names of two more families who have no heat." A part of team one headed over to the Kaminski's on Ames Avenue. Kaminski's would be warm tonight.

Sunday, November 29th, continued to be cold and windy, but throughout that night coal was collected up and down the tracks. The collection area by three o'clock in the morning was extended to Hessville east and to the state line northwest. Everyone anticipated that snow would come by mid-day Monday, so collecting would need to be done before then. It remained bitterly cold. Finally, after 36 hours of continually collecting coal, it was 6:00 Monday morning.

There was now a tired group of young men sitting on old chairs, a rather rickety red table, and the floor around a warm, potbellied stove, drinking half cups of coffee. They were all tired but not yet sleepy. Sleep would come, but right now they were together in good spirits—teammates in their own homemade locker room. They were poor and unemployed, but life had provided them with a full weekend's activities that required their youthful strength—a necessary and important performance that gave them pride—pride that they could see in the eyes and smiling faces of one another and later would see in the eyes of grateful families and friends. Though no one in that moment spoke of God, in their hearts they could feel His caring presence. They had tended to the needs of their fellow man and He was pleased.

But now they would just continue to laugh, talk, and sip their coffee.

Soon any coal that had not been collected would be covered by the coming lake effect storm. The work for their neighbors had been done.

None that early morning would even notice the minuscule dots of lake effect snow beginning to race past the picture window that gave its view of the early dawn over Columbia Avenue.

A Vision of God's Harmony

Our opinions obviously are intimately tied to what we consider to be true. But the beliefs we treasure most we hesitate to talk or write about, for somehow we believe that they are too personal. This having been said, I nonetheless share this personal experience that happened to me long ago. Possibly such has happened also to you.

On the seminary grounds there was a baseball field high on the hill. If you hit a home run over center field, the ball was pretty much gone forever as the drop-off was significant.

But it was mid-December now and quite cold. I stood alone on the highest point of the hill above the baseball field. The sun was beginning to set and the distant sky was filling with magnificent streaks of oranges, blues, and blacks.

It was the last day of a spiritual retreat. For me it was a good retreat. The formal structure helped with that—the total silence, extended time for reflection, the ancient Gregorian chants, the denial of food, the long periods of being alone. As I remember, I didn't at that unaccompanied moment have a particular sense of happiness, but just a sense of peace and inner harmony.

Then it happened. I continued to be by myself but felt no longer alone. I felt as though my entire body, soul, and mind were being held— ever so gently. My gaze remained fixated on the setting sun, but then throughout my total cognitive and emotional being I no longer had any questions. I simply understood. I was in the caring presence of God. There was total and complete cognitive clarity of the entire universe. Everything was so very simple and interrelated. Harmony was in every piece of everything I had ever known and all I had never known. All was part of a whole. It was as if the veil I had unknowingly been wearing all of my life had been momentarily lifted. I could see for the first time and all was in harmony and all was good. I had no answers, for there were no questions. All things were simply understood and part of the whole. Yet there were no parts, simply a whole that was clearly understood. I don't know how long I was there—a thousand years or the minutest part of a second. I could not tell. Time was irrelevant.

And then I was back as suddenly and unexpectedly as it had began.

For fifty years after this experience, I questioned my worthiness to have received it. Finally, it became clear. What I received was a gift, and somehow, for a reason I shall probably never know, God enjoyed giving it. Did I earn it? As I said, it was a gift. Gifts are gifts. They are not wages paid. They are not owed. I know this clearly now, but still I can't get over wanting to someday give something back—not tit for tat, not I owe you one, not it's my turn, but rather just a gift. The way it was given to me—simply because I'd enjoy doing it.

Did I see the face of God that day? I don't think so. I think he just wanted to show me what he had made and have me, in that instant, understand how everything all fits together.

I believe that someday He'll show it to me again. I hope so. I believe He has shown it to many others, and I know that such of His giving is not infrequent. It's just not something most are comfortable talking about. It seems so very personal. I'm sure that some day He will show it to all of us.

I believe it's partially why He created us. He just gets a kick out of sharing things.

Jesse

The young boy watched his father kill his mother and then kill himself with a shotgun. He then sat the whole night near the bodies with his four-year-old brother in his arms. Neighbors found him and his brother the next morning. His name was Jesse, and he was only seven years old.

I met him as he became a seventh-grader. He had just turned 15 and resided at Hoosier Boys Town, a facility for neglected and abused children. I was his teacher and football coach. Though only a year older than his classmates, he was mature beyond his years. He was a handsome young man, tall, wiry, and quick. He had the athletic grace that you find normally only in college athletes. I did not know at that time of his tragic early life. Only later would he tell me of it.

We went undefeated in football that season, and that was in no small way due to the athletic and leadership skills of Jesse. Oh, he didn't win all of those games by himself. I had a talented group—many also from Hoosier Boys Town. I found with these young men that they would do almost anything for you if they felt that you liked them. I really didn't find it hard to form such meaningful bonds. A dear friend,

Dr. Gary Phillips, once told me that with abused and neglected children you will often find that they have what he called, "A hole in the soul," and if you could put your hand gently in that hole, they would be your friend forever.

Football season was over and fall was giving way to light winter snows. Our three-story school was old. My classroom was on the third floor overlooking the playground below. As a teacher you quickly learn that playground activities reveal many things: the bullies, those isolated or ignored, friendship groups and the various leaders. What you tend not to see too often is the student who, though an acknowledged leader, seems simply uninterested in his peers. That was Jesse.

I asked him to stay late one afternoon and we talked. I asked him first why the social distance from his classmates. His answer was straight forward and simple. "Coach, it's not that I don't like them. I'd simply rather not play with the kids." I lamented at how out of place and alone he felt.

He then told me of the early childhood tragedy and of his continuing "night monsters." Afterwards we often took walks. He seemed to like that. We talked many times of many things—things he wanted to share but there was never anyone to listen. Our walks became for both of us special moments. Then on one occasion we visited the high school. As we peered into classrooms, it was as if someone had breathed life into him. He was a different kid. My task was clear. If he agreed, we would try to get him to skip eighth grade and move directly into high school. Later, we met with his Boys Town counselor and principal. We laid out his need to pass the entrance exam. He just sat there, his eyes swelling with tears. Then he said, "I'll pass it." Not long afterwards his counselor called. "Ray thought you would like to know. He has a flashlight in his bed. Pretty sure he studies most of the night."

Jesse passed that test, graduated high school, fought in Viet Nam, married a wonderful girl, and had two children. Some years later, as I was walking out of a class I was teaching at Purdue, I heard from behind me the words of a cherished moment from my past,

"Hey, coach, want to take a walk?"

Maurice

In his early adulthood, Dr Gary Phillips was a coal miner in Southern Indiana. Later, during his prime, he was one of the most accomplished keynote speakers I have ever known. I am honored to say that he became a close friend. I paraphrase now a story he treasured and told so often in his addresses.

Maurice was a handsome, bright boy. He was born in Canada at the beginning of the Great Depression of the 1930s. In school and at home he was often complimented for his scholarly abilities and his inquisitive mind.

As with virtually all children, his early childhood of exploring and tinkering resulted in some splinters and hammered fingers. At school he also seemed to have little aptitude for "hands-on endeavors." By third grade the consensus coming from home and school was clear: Maurice is a very bright and inquisitive boy. An academic path to the future is clear. He should, however, avoid that which requires working with his hands.

With such support and clear direction, Maurice walked the academic path. First, with exceptional academic success at the high school and undergraduate college levels and then graduate work culminating with his doctorate from Harvard. The academic honors were numerous. After his doctorate, Maurice stayed at the university as a researcher and teacher. He moved from assistant professor to associate and, finally, to full professor. He was recognized for his publications and groundbreaking ideas on the nature of human learning. He walked the scholarly path with honor and dignity. Finally, he determined that it was time to retire, enjoy the fruits of his labor, and focus upon his growing grandchildren.

It was in those days of retirement that Maurice found that his most valued moments were taking his grandchildren to the ocean and watching them enjoy the sand and never-ending ocean waves. One of those days as he sat on the beach, his youngest grandson kept bringing to him sticks and ocean-soaked pieces of wood. He found one of these wooden gifts quite intriguing. He liked its unfinished but interesting look. Rather than take it home, he shoved it under the log upon which he sat. Days later, equipped with a pocket knife from his youth, he sat on that log and carefully began to whittle that captivating piece of drift wood.

It would take many days, but eventually it began to take the form and shape of what his mind's eye thought it could be. He liked it. He put it in his coat pocket. He took it home. He showed it only to his wife and then placed it on his bedroom dresser—a display for himself alone.

Some months later, one of his party house guests, while looking for a bathroom, wandered into his bedroom. He spotted the driftwood piece and was taken with its beauty and uniqueness. He was struck particularly by its unique captivating lines. He assumed the cost must be at least equal to its look and asked Maurice where he had purchased it. Maurice sheepishly declared that he was the creator of the piece and insisted on its amateurish quality. His humble expressions were politely discounted. He heard only from his friends, "Would you do one for me?"

Maurice thereafter continued to whittle, enjoying his grandchildren, the ocean, and the sound of the waves.

His creations have been displayed at showings in Vancouver, Canada, Sidney, Australia, San Francisco, and New York.

Of course, as you know, he can't work with his hands.

The Fruits of Trust

I was moving to a new superintendency. Colleagues advised against it. They warned that teacher union leadership there was hostile. Against all advice, I accepted the offer.

When I arrived, threats of strike were in the air. Eventually, a one-year contract was agreed to just in time to move to a new round of negotiations. These years were brutal. I was confidentially advised that the hostility I was experiencing could be traced directly to the former superintendent's public statement, "Union leaders are not very bright. They should have known that I had a full additional percentage to bargain with. They settled for less than what they might have secured."

I asked administrators to adopt the demeanor of peaceful non-aggression. Despite this, hostility continued. It seemed that it was time to plead for a halt. Therefore, during a very tense teacher/administrator meeting, I blurted out, "I don't know who you were married to before but I'm not that person." The room grew silent.

Then Stu, the long time leader of the teachers' association, pulled from his wallet an old faded and warn pay stub of $12.75 that he had received after the strike years ago. He had kept it in his wallet to remind him to never trust administrators. He slowly tore up the pay stub and said, "It's time."

Things changed almost immediately. My associate Dr. Broadwell and I were invited to a "teachers only" bar for a beer. Stu sent word to me that he wanted to consider cooperative bargaining. We selected a highly-regarded Bloomington Indiana attorney, Bob Cambridge, to facilitate.

An appropriate setting was essential, so we rented a retreat center on the Earlham College campus. Each session included catered breakfasts and lunches. Participating teachers were given time off and also substitutes for their classrooms. Our goal was to create contract language that would enhance the dignity and self respect of teachers. Existing boiler plate language would be eliminated. The bargaining was done by teachers, administrators, and board members. In late mornings and early afternoons, clusters of bargainers could be seen gathered in grassy areas among the large trees working on various contract language sections.

A section called "Bereavement" read as follows: "Teachers are permitted five days of absence for the death of a parent, spouse, child or grandparent and two days for a close relative, close to be determined by the personnel director. Deaths of any others will not warrant paid days." That language was changed to: "When a loved one dies, and you decide who a loved one is, then take the time you need."

When bargaining concluded, everyone knew that something special had occurred. That last day I stood by a fence with Stu, as we watched some horses graze. We didn't speak—didn't have to.

Years later, I was keynoting a conference in Atlanta. In the first row were teachers and administrators from my old school district.

I asked, "What are you doing here?"

"We came to hear you. Would you tell them the story of our bereavement language? Since its adoption, no one has ever taken more than five days."

I replied, "But they can."

"No, Dr. Golarz, we will never give to a new superintendent or school board any reason to change what we fashioned with our hearts."

At Stu's funeral his mother gave me his obituary. She said, "Though he led the teacher strike in earlier years, he wanted you to have his obituary. With you he led teachers in the district's first cooperative bargaining process. That was his forever, deep source of pride."

Some thirty years later in a negotiating session, a host of new teachers were offered a wage increase if they would agree to eliminate the bereavement language section from their contract.

They refused.

Little Mary

Occasionally, when I worked in Arkansas, we would drive to one of several elementary schools in the Delta. I always enjoyed such work. Who wouldn't enjoy the trusting simplicity and innocence of these primary children? During these times, I had occasion to work with a third grade child named Mary. Mary was one of seven children. She lived in an old, decrepit structure nearly a mile from her school. Her family had a large rain barrel on the side of the structure. This was the family's source of drinking water and water to clean with. In the dry season the river near the house provided such. Life was oftentimes harsh.

The first time I met with Mary was in the fall. Her teacher told me that Mary had virtually no skill or even a basic understanding of math. Thus, my challenge was to assist Mary with math.

Our first conversation went something like this.

"I understand that your name is Mary. My name is Mister G. Would you mind if I help you with your math?"

Mary replied. "That's up to you, but ya need to understand it's been tried before."

"Well, Mary, can I try?"

"Sure, but you got to understand that it's in the blood. My mother and grandmother couldn't do math either—it's in the blood, ya see. Mamma told me it's in the blood, but if you want to try, go ahead." My work with Mary on that first day was fruitless except for, I believe, her beginning to like me.

Several weeks later, during the second visit, I got an unanticipated break. As Mary and I were beginning to work, I dropped five or six coins from my pocket while attempting to secure a handkerchief. Mary began to pick up the coins and as she did she said, "Can you help me to understand what these mean? All the other kids know what they mean and it's embarrassing for me." I had an opening and I took it. The various denominations of coins would be my vehicle. For the next several hours we worked slowly and patiently. She was beginning to learn. As we concluded I said to her. "You're getting to understand this, aren't you?'

She smiled and responded, "It could be just one of those things." She wasn't ready to acknowledge that she was beginning to understand.

I would work with Mary one more time. By that session's end she could add and subtract using coins nearly as quickly as I could. I said to her, "You're getting to know this, aren't you?" She replied with a sheepish smile, "I have to say yes, Mr. G. cause my momma has told me never to lie, but I don't know math real good yet." I smiled and said, "But you will, Mary, but you will."

Several months later, I received a letter from Mary's teacher. She wanted me to know that Mary had become the math classroom tutor, assisting other children having trouble. She always uses coins as her vehicle to teach. Enclosed in her letter was a note from Mary.

"Mr. G. I am getting' better and I'm helpin' some other kids. Gettin' them to do the math is the easy part. Gettin' them to believe is harder.

Oh, also, me and my momma went shoppin' and when we got done I told momma how much change she should be gettin'. On the way home she asked me if I could teach her how to do that. Mr. G, maybe it ain't in the blood--just maybe."

Mary

Rules for Golf—Rules for Life

The sixteenth hole was a beautiful par three over a pond with tall weeds and cattails around its shores. Golfers completing the fifteenth hole would leave their caddies, take their club of choice and walk the 60 yards to the sixteenth tee. Sixteen was 120 yards long and the green gently sloped toward its back. Many balls fell victim to that slope.

When I was twelve and my brother Joe ten, some young male members of the country club had hired a stripper. The girl, standing on the sixteenth tee, would expose her breasts or raise her skirt as golfers would try to drive from that tee. Joe's golfer decided to have some fun with him, a young caddy. From the sixteenth tee he yelled to Joe to bring him another club. I yelled back as I grabbed the back of Joe's shirt.

"I'll bring it."

He replied, "I said the little guy."

I yelled back. "He ain't comin'."

The tee, filled with golfers, got silent as he screamed, "Send him here."

I screamed back, "Kiss my a**!"

I then grabbed Joe and left the course. The next day, the president of the Country Club Board called Joe and me to the clubhouse. He admonished us and told us we should never again swear or curse at a golfer.

Two weeks later on Tuesday, the women's golf day, I was caddying for Mrs. Crenshaw. She apparently had asked for me. At the end of the golf game as we left the eighteen green and were walking toward the clubhouse, she asked, "Are you the young man who objected to having your little brother go to the vile sixteenth tee?" "Yes ma'am."

"Well, I'm Mrs. Crenshaw, President of the Club's Women's Auxiliary. The young men who initiated that immoral incident on sixteen are no longer members of this country club. They clearly didn't understand our ethical standards and who runs this establishment. You may share that with your fellow caddies." She then looked down at me, smiled and from her flowered change purse handed me an unexpected ten dollar tip.

I loved that eighteenth green not because of the ten dollar tip, but because, in later years as Joe and I were finishing the last round we would ever play on that course, his smile radiated as he lined up his last putt. I believe it was his warm smile that keeps that memory so alive.

We grew up on that country club golf course. I think we grew up in a good way. I believe that the lesson we best learned as we played with poor, but honest fellow caddies and ethical country club members like Mrs. Crenshaw was to never violate the rules.

For a score to be treasured at the end of eighteen holes, you need to know that for all of those holes you never transgressed, you never cheated yourself. And your score in life, like the score on the golf course, is laudable only because you worked at following the rules—all of the rules. Rannulph Junuh (Matt Damon) demonstrated this in the movie *Bagger Vance* when he called a stroke on himself because he unintentionally violated a rule by causing his ball to slightly move. He said, "The ball was here and it rolled to here."

His young caddy objected, "Only you and me seen it. No one will know."

Then Rannulph replied, "I will know, Hardy, and so will you."

Maybe life is best lived when simply played like an honest and ethical game of golf.

Just maybe.

Prayers for a Chosen
Warrior and a Better Life

I had just been offered an opportunity to direct an inner city poverty intervention project I accepted. The depressing nature of my work peaked one snowy, cold, late Friday afternoon in mid-December during my fifth year directing the project.

I was checking on a referral from the court. The referral took me to an apartment in an old mansion built in 1880 that we called "the maze." Rickety staircases lined the outside of the building, and, from a distance, the entire structure had the look of braided hair. Cautiously maneuvering myself up one of the riskily staircases, I found 22B.

I knocked. It opened into a gray, dark, empty, very cold room. Near the back wall was a child about six months old. He was just lying there. His breathing seemed labored. He was wet, shivering, and wearing nothing more than a very soiled diaper. I yelled, but no one responded. I knocked on other apartment doors—no response. I removed the child's soiled wet diaper then wrapped him in my coat and left a note, "Have your baby. Come to Police Department."

All the way to the Police Department I couldn't get the picture of the apartment out of my mind—endless shades of gray. I thought of my own children's bedroom—so different.

As I drove, I held my hand on the child lying next to me, a child clearly trying to breathe between deep coughs. At the station, Sgt. Wleklinski, one of my mentors, met me. We had worked together so many times before.

He took one look at the baby and then said, "You know Chicago Police that can get us into South Chicago Hospital's pediatric emergency center?"

I responded, "Yes." "Then, do it. Do it now. Do it quickly."

All the way over to the Skyway through the rapid flashing red and blue lights of the squad car, all I could envision as I held the child now gasping for breath, were endless shades of gray. Poverty and deprivation create some indelible images

Next morning about 7:00 A.M., Wleklinski called me at home. With a trembling voice, he told me that the hospital had just called and despite their best efforts, the little guy didn't make it. He was dehydrated too long. There was too much pneumonia, too much fever, just too much of everything for the little guy. I thanked him for calling and hung up. I walked to the open doorway of my own children's bedroom. They were all still asleep.

As I stood there watching them with my head leaning against the door frame, a tear ran down my cheek and then several more. I didn't want to cry, but it wasn't going to be something I would decide. There are times when it happens that way. And inside of you, it just hurts.

Several weeks later Wliklinski called. "Ray?" "Yeah." "We located that little guy's mother. Seems she was having a back alley abortion the day you found her little guy. She didn't make it. The fetus, a girl, didn't make it either. Thought you would like to know. She was 14, just a kid herself. Ray, I don't know how much more of this I can handle, really getting to me—can't seem to turn it off, not really sleeping well. Sometimes I think being a cop is just pure hell."

That night I lay in my bed, eyes open, and said some prayers. First for Wliklinski who, though he would never admit it, was one of God's chosen warriors given to us to be here in the most difficult of times where without him our own courage would be inadequate.

And then a prayer for a young mother and her two kids. I asked God to please give them a better life up there. They didn't get one down here-so very many don't ever get much down here.

Charlie

I was nearing my fifth birthday. My dad, Lefty, and I were in my grandfather's back yard. Dad was searching through the woodpile, for he was doing some carpentry work. I was sitting on the top of the wood pile—a favorite kid's spot.

"Dad, I have a new friend"

"Who, son?"

"Well, you know across the street from our house, past the brickyard and close to the coal yard?"

"Yeah."

"Well, there's a black kid there my size. We played yesterday. His uncle from Chicago came by when we were playin' and asked me who I was. I told him, and he wanted to know if I was Lefty's kid. I said "yes." Said he had played football with you and that you and he had been good friends—told me to tell you that Charlie said. "Hi."

"You remember him?"

"Sure do. We grew up together in this neighborhood."

"What was he like, Dad?"

"He was the fastest kid I have ever known. But more importantly, on a football field he could change directions without losing speed."

"Is that good, Dad?"

"It sure is son. Had he been given the ball every play and then had good blocking, our team would have gone undefeated."

"Did he carry the ball a lot?"

"No."

"Why?"

"Because he was black."

"I don't understand, Dad."

"Ray, just because you're the best, doesn't mean that this world is going to give you what you deserve—especially if you're black. Once in practice, Charlie ran up the middle for a great gain and then lots of players piled on him. When my brother Walt and I got to the pile, we could hear Charlie screaming. We started pulling guys off. When we got to him, we could see that he had huge bite marks all over his legs and arms. We pulled him up and he stood there between Walt and me, shaking."

"What did you do?"

"With Charlie between us, we told those guys that if anything like that ever happened again to Charlie, we would come into their neighborhood, find them, and beat the s*** out of them right on the street in front of their neighbors and families."

"Did you do it?"

"Didn't have to."

"Why?"

"It never happened again."

"Why?"

"They knew we meant it."

Dad then stopped and just stared for a long moment quietly in the direction of our apartment and the coal yard beyond. Then he said, "Son, climb down from that wood pile. You and an old friend who's visiting some of his family deserve a proper introduction."

Later that afternoon Dad introduced me to his friend Charlie. I said, "Hello Mr. Charlie," shook hands, and then went off to play with my new friend in the brickyard. Dad and Charlie sat on the front steps of an old house nearest the coal yard just talking and drinking a couple of beers.

God provides for immense learning if a kid has a woodpile and an honest and noble dad.

Treasure the Chance Moments

I was invited to keynote a criminal justice conference in Miami. For reasons I still don't understand, Marion could not go, and my Dad became the unplanned replacement.

I can still remember Marion's words, "Why don't you take your Dad?"

I said, "Do you think he could handle the trip?"

"Take a chance. He and you might both enjoy it."

I called Dad. There was no question about his excitement. He even said that he would bring some golf balls and tees just in case. We were going to Miami.

Dad had never lost his innocence and love of life. In the plane he wanted the window seat. No six-year-old's excitement could hold a candle to his enthusiasm as he looked out of the window. When we got to our hotel, we found that our room had an ocean view. He loved that view as well as the sound of the waves.

At 5:45 A.M. I was awakened by heavy breathing coming from the direction of Dad's bed. Could he be having a heart attack? I looked in his direction. He wasn't in his bed. He was between our beds doing push-ups. He smiled and just said. "Hey kid, it's going to be a great day." I was stunned.

The following day, after my keynote address, we found that the hotel had an agreement with a golf course. Guests could play for free. When we arrived at the golf course, we could not have been more impressed. It was called the Doral. We entered the pro shop and got in line to secure a tee time-Dad with his cut off Bermuda shorts, pipe between his teeth, and a plastic bag in his hand containing our golf balls and tees. I was standing next to him wearing my Chicago Cubs baseball cap above the red bandana around my neck. We were strictly class—cover of GQ. It was clear that our presence provoked a resounding hush. Finally, Dad said to me in his base-baritone voice, "Hey kid, look at all the clothes for sale in here, looks like a department store."

When we finally got to the counter, Dad thumped his bag of golf balls and tees on the glass counter. You could cut the tension with a dull knife.

"Sir, how can I help you?"

Dad replied, "Just need a tee time, young fella, we're from the hotel."

The clerk responded with obvious and observable relief, "Sir, your golf course is two miles away. Just go out our main gate and take a left."

We found our course as he suggested. We entered the grounds slowly, for there were many potholes from recent rains—definitely our kind of place. Dad was a fairly good golfer as was I. In years past we had put up some extremely respectable scores. Today, however, was just going to be fun. Our drives dribbled off of the tee. Further, we played more frequently in the roughs than the fairways, and we lost a lot of our golf balls. When down to two, we made a new rule: find a golf ball on the course, and you can take a stroke off your score. We laughed a lot that day and enjoyed each other's camaraderie. Later in the clubhouse over some beers, we laughed some more.

Dad is gone now and I miss him so. But when I think back on that chance trip, I smile. So my friends, if ever you are presented with such an opportunity with your parent don't pass it by.

It will be a treasure no one can ever take from you. And that eventual smile on your face will belong to you and him or her alone.

Danny and Michael

D anny came to my seventh grade class from foster care, placed in
the school district with a loving family. He could neither read nor
write. He was a tall, gangly, timid boy. I did not know of his deficiencies
until he handed in his first in-class writing assignment. What he handed
in was a page filled with lines of scribbling, blank space, more scribbling,
blank space, more scribbling, blank space, on and on, line after line.
There were no words. My heart ached. It ached more as I observed him
at recess preferring to play with first and second graders. His foster
parents, the principal, and I met. We did not conclude with a viable
plan, merely a commitment to find one.

Several days later on a rainy fall morning when the "walkers" were
permitted early entry into the school building, I observed Danny sitting
on a stair with a classmate, Michael. Michael was short and overweight,
extremely shy, and very bright. Yet, as shy as Michael was and as timid
as Danny was, they appeared to be enjoying their conversation and
moment of camaraderie. I had been praying for an opportunity, and
God, who I believe sits on the shoulder of all teachers was saying,
"Here's your opening. Take it and run." I didn't need to be told twice.

After school that same day, knowing that they were both "walkers," I asked them to assist me in taking equipment to the park football practice field three blocks away. They both responded "Sure Coach, we'd like to." They talked all the way to the park, completely ignoring my presence.

A second writing assignment came several weeks later. I advised Danny that he did not need to do it. He looked up at me and said, "Coach, if I can find a way to do it, will you take it?" I said, "Sure, Danny. Sure." The day the assignment, was due, Michael and Danny came to me. Michael turned in his assignment and then the two of them handed me another paper. Michael explained, "For a week Danny has been making up this story and memorizing it. Yesterday, I wrote it for him. He knows he can't write yet. But, it is his story. Will you take it?" I kept that paper for many years. It was so very elegant in its simplicity.

I knew Michael wanted to do something athletic so, I would regularly give the two of them a basketball and let them go out on the playground's far end for twenty minutes or so to practice. Eventually, they would come to me after school to get the basketball and play until dark.

A wonderful memory I still have is looking out of my third floor classroom window and watching the two of them, arm over arm, walking home in the twilight of evening.

Michael got pretty good at basketball. He was hard to beat at horse. Danny with mostly Michael's help learned to write. When Danny and his wife had their first child, they selected Michael and His wife as their daughter's godparents.

Their friendship was life-long.

Joe Went to Alaska

Bill, the President of the teachers association, came to my office. "Ray, I have a request."

He then continued. "You know Jack Nelson—biology teacher at Central high school?"

"Vaguely."

"Well, Jack and I go way back, actually started teaching together some 38 years ago. He was some crackerjack teacher in those days— fire in the belly. You couldn't get him to stop talking about biology— even over a beer. Things change though. Eventually, if you teach long enough, no one even remembers your name or what you teach. So you tire.

In Jack's early years he had a dream. He wanted to go to Alaska and take pictures and then produce slides of the flora and fauna for his classes. Well, several of Jack's close friends are going to Alaska on a hunting trip this coming September, and they have asked Jack to come along with his cameras. But Jack's personal leave time is all used up. He used it when his wife was hospitalized. Ray, would you meet with

Jack and several of us from the association to see if we can help him?"
I agreed.

Later, we met after school in my office—association leadership, Jack, and I. Jack explained his situation. We deliberated. Our deliberation was resolving nothing. The peaceful meeting was becoming tense. Jack politely got up and headed for the door.

He turned and said, "I'm sorry, I didn't mean to cause such a problem."

I then said something I had not planned. To this day I can only assume that I was guided in my statement by a power greater than me. "Jack wait. I have four unused personal days. Take mine." We were all stunned, including me.

I turned to Bill. "Will the contract let me do this, Bill?"

Bill slowly replied. "I'm not sure. Let us look into it."

They left shortly thereafter. Several days later Bill called, "Ray we won't need your days, but need your assistance. We the association leadership have decided to add a new provision to our contract permitting teachers to exchange unused personal leave days. Will you take this to the school board so that they can sign off on it?"

"Be happy to Bill."

Jack went to Alaska with his friends. He did so with five personal leave days given to him by teaching colleagues. He took his pictures of the flora and fauna and created his set of slides. After his return, our school board president asked him to present a portion of his slides at a school board meeting. His presentation was fascinating. He ended with these words. "It's been very long since my work has been so honored. Thank you."

Some say that Jack's last two years of teaching were his best. He taught with a "fire in the belly" that captivated his students and brought rookie teachers to him for guidance.

According to Peter Drucker, as reported in *Definitive Drucker,* an organization's potential for greatness can only be found in the hearts of those who work there assuming that they can answer "yes" to the following:

Are you given the things you need so that you can make a contribution?

Do people notice that you did it?

Finally, are you treated with respect and dignity?

Isn't that the way God would want it?

"Until We Meet Again"

In the movie, *Heaven is for Real*, a boy dies and goes to heaven. He later tells his mother about things he experienced.

"Mom, I didn't know I had a sister. "

"Of course you do, she's right here."

"No, the one that died in your tummy. I met her in heaven."

"What was her name?"

"She didn't have a name. You and dad didn't have time to name her. Oh, there was a beautiful horse in heaven too."

"A horse?"

"Sure, mom. Heaven's full of animals, all kinds."

For many who saw this movie, it's a sweet fantasy. But for me, a hopeless romantic, if I can believe in millions of angels dancing on the head of a pin, then I can certainly believe that miscarried babies and also dogs and cats go to heaven.

Marion and I never owned a cat—dogs-a-plenty. Then, one late afternoon when we were driving home on a very dark and wooded county road, a shaggy, flea bitten, scrawny white kitten appeared. We stopped and Marion opened the door. Without hesitation he shot into the car. We had a cat. He was lucky that we saw him and picked him up, so we named him Lucky. We got him to the vet, fed him and cleaned him. He never really ever became totally domesticated, but then neither have I. He seemed a good fit. When we unintentionally forgot his food or water he would gently nip Marion in her Achilles heel. Within two years, every one of our adult married children owned a cat.

Patches came to us a couple of years later. She was the runt of a litter from the shelter—a pretend calico. She was sick when we brought her home. For a month she sat next to me in my recliner. Once she was well, she would sleep whenever she could on Marion's lap or on a bed in the afternoon sun. When wanting to be held, she would follow Marion around the house and meow sharply until picked up. She was the greatest of animals. Never full-sized, she conversed with you with her eyes that were always so full of life and pixy sparkle. I personally believe God gives us babies and these little animals so that while on earth we can experience pure honesty, trust, and openness.

Lucky, after 17 years, found a remote place in the attic to pass away. Patches never really stopped looking for him. Several years later Patches suddenly wouldn't eat. We actually attempted to feed her with a toothpick and ground up tuna. The medical diagnosis was terrifying—inoperable tumor and increasing pain.

When you get to my age, you have seen death and dying—friends, relatives, and animals. But it is most overwhelming when you are the ones deciding when the end will come. She rested in Marion's arms, purring and looking up at me with her gentle eyes. After the vet's second shot, she continued to look up but the purring had stopped and gone was the pixy sparkle. We sat quietly holding her for a very long time.

Some day when it is our time, we will head upwards, God willing, and as we gaze out over God's bliss, we will find both of them. It will be quite easy. For you see, Marion will hear sharp meows and feel something nipping her Achilles. We will turn, look down, then peer into their gentle pixy sparkling eyes.

You may believe what you wish, but for us, God just doesn't let innocent and pure things simply die.

Choctaw Warrior

On a small sharecropper farm in Oklahoma, a boy of the Choctaw tribe was born. He would become a warrior and my friend. His name was Don Sims. I first met Don at a conference in Phoenix. Rarely had I met anyone so enthusiastic. We talked until early morning of ways to help children. He invited me to his reservation and to the Riverside Indian School in Oklahoma.

On my first visit he took me to a large field near the center of the reservation.

He said, "Ray, there will be a basketball gym here and shortly thereafter, my Indian students will honor themselves in the basketball state tournament. "

I said, "When do you start construction?"

He laughed and said, "Don't know yet, don't have the money."

Six years later, the Riverside Indian students went to the final four.

The dropout rate in Indian schools is horrific. So, Don started a school for dropouts. But unlike other dropout schools, his school would have no semesters or other such traditional barriers. Each enrolled student would take whatever time they needed in each course of study. In its first year, Don's school graduated over 100 students.

After Riverside, Don accepted the challenge of Sherman Indian School in California, a school representing students from over 80 native tribes. By Don's second year, he and his teachers made a modification to the report card. The report card would have a new grade designation, NY (not yet). Failure would not be an option, for students would be given whatever time they needed. Time would become a variable.

Several years later, Don created and then held a first of its kind all tribes Powwow. It was a Powwow involving many of the tribal members representing Sherman. Around the evening fire, the children and many chiefs of the Sioux, Navaho, Fox, Cherokee, Apache, and others danced in their traditional attire. As the fire waned, the princess of the powwow was presented. Don, with permission of tribal elders, asked that I dance with her. It was for me an honor and now a cherished memory.

My visits became more infrequent but always so very uplifting, for whenever arriving at his office, it was always filled with native students. I asked him once why this unusual openness.

He simply replied, "They need this and, I guess, so do I."

Then, some years later, in a phone conversation, the first seven minutes or so of the conversation he seemed very distant and confused. It didn't feel like I was talking to my friend. Finally, he exclaimed excitedly, "Ray!" We talked only a few minutes more. I somehow knew that my friend was only temporarily back. When we ended our call, I knew that I would not be talking to my friend again in this lifetime. It was very clear that the memory of me was fading. I sat, wept, and prayed in respectful silence.

In earlier years we half-jokingly kidded that when we neared the end of this life we would go to Eagle Nest Butte and share a pipe. I would have liked that. I think he would have too. The Choctaw recognize death as a new journey.

So I say, "Journey on good friend. Be in harmony with nature, and be with **Nanishta**—God of the Choctaw. We will try to follow the path here that you left for us. It is the path of an honored Choctaw warrior—God's gift to us of such warriors as you is rare."

Studying the Stars

M ost teachers and school administrators were ordained before birth to teach. Such was the case of Joe Grayson and his teachers. Their focus was to do everything they could for students. I was an assistant superintendent when I got Joe's call.

"Ray, can you come out to our school and meet with several teachers?"

"Sure Joe, when?"

"Any chance you can come today?"

"See you after school, Joe."

At 4:30 P.M., I met with Joe and five teachers.

Joe began, "Ray, we have a young man, age 16 preparing to drop out of school and work at Standard Foundry. We, however, all think he has incredible academic potential. With this in mind, we have created an unorthodox educational experience that we think will keep him in school. Mr. Nelson our physics teacher will explain."

"Dr. Golarz, the boy's name is Richard and his family is quite poor. With money he has saved working at Wleklinski's bowling alley, he is completing the construction of a four-inch reflector telescope in his basement. He ground his own lens and his work is flawless. He would like to add timing mechanisms to follow stars across the night-sky, but he currently lacks that skill.

We want to form an interdisciplinary curricular team and assist his growth. After he has completed the construction of the telescope with the functional timing mechanisms, he will have to demonstrate that he has met the curricular standards set by the state. To achieve this end, Mrs. Jones, our English teacher, would work with him in the design and preparation of a thesis paper. I would assess his understanding of the physics implications. Mr. Jennings would guide his understanding of the historical aspects related to the development of telescopes. Mr. Thomas would consult regarding the mathematical considerations. And finally, Miss Zerrig would help him prepare a speech, for later he will be required to orally present his work.

I then said, "I assume that this is where I come in." They all smiled.

My task was not as difficult as you might imagine At the time, I was working with a school board which was three standard deviations left of center, so they readily agreed to anything that was challenging and adventuresome. In addition, I knew several high-ranking state department administrators who made the board appear conservative.

Once the semester began, all seemed to go as clockwork. Then in mid October, there was an unanticipated glitch. A critical part of the telescope timing mechanism would not function half way into an event series. All pitched in and worked around the clock, but the problem was beyond the capacities of all of us, including both Mr. Nelson and Mr. Thomas. Therefore, Mr. Thomas and Richard contacted the Planetarium in Chicago. They explained everything and were then invited to come to Chicago for a session with two of the planetarium's astronomers. They were to bring the homemade telescope and all related equipment.

The rest was incredible. The unanticipated glitch gave Richard an opportunity to share his work and his passion. The astronomers loved Richard. They loved his enthusiasm, his work ethic, and his commitment to know. The teachers that he would interact with now would include two of the planetarium's staff. Each Wednesday he would catch an early morning South Shore train and spend the day in Chicago "studying the stars."

Ultimately, Richard completed his project. His oral presentation was stunning. That Christmas he began his lifelong study, practice, and years later the teaching of astronomy. An unexpected glitch had changed the course of what might have been—a glitch that no one could ever account for.

Maybe our Lord just decided that He needed another enthusiastic astronomer to study His stars.

The Advocate

I had just finished participating in a case conference the purpose of which was to rewrite an IEP (individualized educational plan) for a special needs fourth-grader in our school system. After the conference I asked Martha (the boy's mother) to join me in my office. Besides representing her son, Martha advocated for many of the districts children. She had an in depth understanding of special education law and a profound sensitivity for special needs children.

Resources available for special needs children have always been inadequate. From the early 1970s the special education mandate has never been adequately funded. Martha, besides advocating for individual children, always helped me with the legislature and funding issues. She was tireless in this regard. We met that afternoon and plotted some legislative strategies for the coming general assembly session. As we completed our work, I asked Martha if she would mind a personal question.

She nodded and said, "Go ahead, Ray."

So I said, "Martha, you are a truly extraordinary advocate and you have the persistence of a junkyard dog. Can you help me understand the source of your endless zeal?"

She looked at me for a long moment and then asked, "Ray, do you mind if I close the door."

I said, "No, of course not."

She then began. "If a child's special needs are not clearly identified, we tend to assume he is normal and treat the child accordingly. My son Timmy seemed normal. So when Timmy transgressed we assumed that he was being defiant or stubborn. By the time he was six dealing with him alone took ten times the effort and strength needed to deal with our other children. Jack left for work early each morning and typically didn't get home until 6:00 P.M. By evening each day I was exhausted. If I hadn't slept the night before, I was a zombie. On one of those days I had reached my limit. I grabbed Timmy by his shoulders and then screamed at him. I said, 'Get out, leave this house, go away and don't come back.'

When I regained my composure, I began to prepare supper. The house seemed unusually quiet. Then some instinct told me to look for Timmy. So I did. I looked everywhere but could not find him. Panic set in, and I went outside searching the neighborhood, now screaming out his name. When Jack got home, I gave him a brief explanation then took his car.

It was beginning to sleet. The car was sliding as I braked on freezing streets. I was making bigger and bigger circles on streets away from our home. I finally got to the boulevard. Traffic was heavy. Standing on the corner was this sad and pathetic six-year-old with a stick on his shoulder and cans of food at the end of the stick wrapped in a bathroom towel.

I jumped from the car, leaving it in the street, and screamed 'Timmy.'

He looked up at me and said through his tears, 'I am so sorry, Mommy. I did what you said and left but I don't know where to go.'

I grabbed him and hugged and held him. As I knelt there holding him, I vowed to God that I would never again hurt him—nor would I ever let anyone else hurt him, nor would I allow any special child to be hurt.

A month later, we got his psychological evaluation that included a listing of the behaviors over which he most likely had no control." She said no more. She didn't have to.

God selects His advocates quite wisely.

A Calling

School superintendents spend a great deal of their time dealing with unpleasant tasks. That's why they like to visit primary classrooms. Young children are always so enthusiastic and happy. The personnel department is also an uplifting place to visit, for you will often find teachers new to the profession waiting to see if they can be hired. One late summer day I wandered down to that office hoping to be uplifted.

"Dr. Golarz, good to see you here."

"Thanks. What are you doing?"

"Well, we're attempting to hire a third grade teacher and we are down to two finalists. Want to help?"

"Love to."

"Well, we will send the candidates to you as soon as you complete reviewing their files."

I was really quite excited. The selection of a new teacher is such an awesome responsibility. I opened the first file. I found page after page of outstanding academic work plus a record of many honors and awards. I asked my staff to send in the candidate.

"Young man, would you mind if I asked you a few questions?"

"Sure, go ahead."

"Why do you want to work here?"

"Well, you're not my first choice, but until those other schools have an opening I will help you out for a year. I know I'm over qualified for your district, but a year is not too long."

I was stunned—almost speechless. The remainder of the interview went downhill. After he left, I sat for a long moment trying to regroup.

I then opened the second file. I moved from page to page but came up empty. Finally I closed the file and asked staff to send her in.

She sat and I said, "Do you mind if I get right to the heart of this?" She replied. "No, not at all."

So I said. "You didn't do too well in college, did you?"

She smiled, chuckled a bit and said, "That's an understatement."

I then said, "I know you must have, at minimum, a GPA of 2.0 or you couldn't have received a diploma."

She replied, "Yep, that was my GPA, a solid 2.0."

I then said. "Why do you think we should hire you?"

"Well, I know my record looks bad—took me six years to finish. I often had to work two jobs to make it, but I never quit. You see, I had some great teachers and for some reason I have felt from the time I was a little girl that I had a calling to be a teacher. Also, I love kids, even the tough and mean ones."

Well, we got to talking. Half an hour slipped by. Eventually, almost an hour. I then looked at her and said, "You know, I like you." She smiled and responded, "I like you too. Who are ya?" I said, "I'm the superintendent." She laughed and replied, "I like you anyway."

Finally, I said, "I'm going to recommend that we hire you. I have a feeling that you are just what we need."

In early October I called Nancy, her principal.

"Nancy, can I come over and observe her teach?"

"You come over any time. You'll get a kick out of this," and then she said, "We all love her—she has a rare gift for teaching."

The next morning I slipped into the back of her classroom. I was taken aback for she was teaching a relatively sophisticated piece of mathematics. Before I left, I had her join me in the hallway and I said somewhat jokingly, "I didn't think you knew that stuff." She beamed and sassily replied, "I don't. We're learning it together."

Three years later her colleagues voted her teacher of the year.

None of us found this surprising. From the time she was a little girl she had been called. Remember?

Maybe God Saw a
Different Need

I t was a spectacular spring day. Over the previous two weeks we had gotten more than our fair share of mid-America rain, so the grass that had been waiting all winter was growing, touched everywhere by spring flowers. As I looked out of my office door that morning, I could see Johnny, the Director of Buildings and Grounds, walking briskly through the sun-filled hallway.

I asked, "Johnny, found that portable classroom yet?"

I was having a little fun with him. We had twelve portable one-room classrooms that we moved around to different locations in the school district as enrollments shifted and we found a need for additional space. Last year we had been using ten of the portables. Two were sitting idle. Well, one was sitting idle. The whereabouts of the second was unknown.

In the school business you get used to having some things occasionally disappear: library books, a computer, cables needed for electronic equipment, a basketball, baseball equipment, even once a fairly sizable, portable soccer backstop—but a portable classroom? Never lost a portable classroom.

I knew it was a sensitive spot for Johnny, so I let up, laughed and said, "Johnny, don't worry. We'll find it. I mean, really. How far can you get with a hot portable? Where could you possibly hide it and how would you fence it?" I laughed again. Johnny just looked up and shook his head.

A week or so later, Johnny and I were visiting some of our elementary schools in the central city. We were trying to get into as many classrooms as we could. Teachers never get enough visitors. When they do, they never tire of having their pupils show off regarding something that they had just learned. As superintendent, I always found it to be an uplifting experience. We left the last school on our list of morning visits, got into our car, and as we drove around the school grounds, we marveled at the manicured lawn and beautiful flower beds. The flowers surrounding the new parent center behind the school were particularly well-tended. The new parent center—what an attractive, wonderful welcome gift to the poor parents of this community.

We stopped on the street for a moment of admiration. As we sat there, not looking at one another, Johnny asked, "Ray, what would you estimate the size of that freshly painted, one-room parent center, surrounded by beautiful flowers to be?"

"You mean is it possible that the parent center with the flower boxes under the windows and new white gutters and down spouts is about the same size as a missing classroom portable?"

We parked the car and went into the building to find Nancy, the principal. On the way to her office we ran into her. "Oh, I'm so glad you're here, Ray. Have you time to stop at the parent center?"

"Nancy, that's what we need to talk to you about? Can we go to your office?"

"Sure, or we can talk at the parent center. It's not as full now as it is in the morning. Can't even find elbow room in there in the mornings."

"Full? What are you talking about, Nancy?"

"Well, we opened the center about six weeks ago. Within a week, by 6:30 A.M. it was full of young mothers. They found out that a number of our teachers were coming in early to teach a few mothers how to read. Well, they all wanted to learn to read. Run three morning classes now, an hour each, starting at 5:00 A.M., about twenty in a class. Teachers rotate the teaching of the classes."

"They come at 5:00 A.M.?"

"Some would come earlier if we were open. If they stay at home, their drunken exes or boyfriends coming in from the bars look to have their way with them, raping them if they don't consent. It's a bad situation in this neighborhood for these young women and their kids. Bad, Ray—really bad. Poor is not a good thing to be in America. I've had young mothers weep in my arms and bless us for being here. Several said that they had been praying for such help and had nearly given up hope just before we opened. But, I'm so sorry. Here I am running off at the mouth, and you wanted to talk to me about something."

I looked at Johnny, then turned to her and said, "It can wait, Nancy. It can wait."

We had our visit at the new parent center, even enjoyed doughnuts made by a few of the teachers. As we passed by the center in our car, we stopped for a final look.

"What do you think, Johnny?"

Johnny quietly responded, "Think the portable we're lookin' for is smaller. Matter of fact, I'm sure it's smaller."

I looked at Johnny, smiled, nodded my head slowly and responded, "Think you're right, Johnny. Think you're right."

A *little* Leftover Prayer

In the story *Choctaw Warrior* that you read earlier in the book I spoke of my friend Don Sims. As a final note to this book I would like to relay a short story that Don told to me.

Don headed up Riverside Indiana School in Oklahoma for many years. Not infrequently an abandoned young Indian child would show up at the school. One very late, cold October night Gangii, a Navaho child showed up. After they cleaned him up and fed him, Don took him to one of the dormitories for younger children.

Don personally took him to a room assigned to him with three roommates and his own bed. It was quite late and his roommates were asleep, so Don whispered to him to get into his bed, say his prayers, and go to sleep. Gangii, quite tired, quickly got into bed. Don said that he then went into the hallway close to Gangii's open door. He waited a moment and then heard him say.

"God, I'm Gangii and I'm really tired and I don't remember that whole prayer to you. But you're God, and I know you know it. So if you don't mind, could you say it tonight for me? I promise that tomorrow I will try to say it with you."

Don said that he teared up and tried to walk quietly back down the hallway. Then he said to me, "God, I love my Indian kids."

About the Author

Raymond J Golarz holds his B.A. and B.S. degrees from St. Joseph's College in Indiana. In addition he received his M.S. and Ed.D. Degrees from Indiana University. He taught as a middle school and high school teacher and then served as the Director of Child Welfare Services supervising delinquency prevention and intervention programs and working with delinquent gangs and directing drug intervention programs.

At the college level, he taught an array of psychology courses at St. Joseph's college, Purdue Calumet, Indiana University Northwest and City College in Seattle. For ten years he taught Psychology for law enforcement officers near Chicago to hundreds of law enforcement officers.

He has served as an assistant superintendent and superintendent of schools and has keynoted conferences in virtually every Canadian Province as well as almost every state in the United States. Currently, Ray does work as a newspaper columnist featured in Yahoo news, USA Today and the Bloomington Herald Times while his wife Marion continues work as a content editor.

With Marion his wife of 56 years he has co-authored *The Power of Participation, Sweet Land of Liberty,* and *the Problem Isn't Teachers.* In addition, he has co-authored *Restructuring Schools for Excellence through Teacher Empowerment* and is the author of *On My Way Home I Bumped into God.* His earlier writings include *Yellow Jacket Football in Hard Times and Good* and a companion book *When the Yellow Jackets Played,* two books focusing on the strengths of the early immigrants who came to America.

He and Marion have six children: Tanya Scherschel, Michael Golarz, Scott Golarz, Jocelyn Morris, Daniel Golarz and Thomas John Golarz and they presently have eleven grandchildren. They reside in Bloomington, Indiana with their calico cat Nola and their Boxer dog Cooper.

All of his life Ray has enjoyed sketching, oil painting, and carpentry. The final enjoyment of carpentry he considers a gift from his father and grandfathers.

As a consequence of his keynoting, he has been given many special gifts. His most prized possession is the White Buffalo Indian Robe given to him after keynoting the National Native American School Boards Convention.

He can be contacted at their email address:
mjgolarz@live.com

Printed in the United States
by Baker & Taylor Publisher Services